In The Name of Love

The Asteroid Psyche

Anne-Marie Chabellard

THE WESSEX ASTROLOGER

Published in 2026 by The Wessex Astrologer Ltd
PO Box 9307
Swanage
BH19 9BF
England

For a full list of our titles go to www.wessexastrologer.com

© Anne-Marie Chabellard
Anne-Marie Chabellard asserts her moral right to be recognised as the author of this work

ISBN: 9781916625426

Cover design by Fiona Bowring at Bowring Creative
Typeset by Kevin Moore

A catalogue record for this book is available at The British Library

No part of this book may be reproduced or used in any form or by any means without the written permission of the publisher. Without limiting the exclusive rights of any author, contributor, or the publisher of this publication, any unauthorised use of this publication to train generative artificial intelligence (AI) technologies is expressly prohibited.
A reviewer may quote brief passages.

Table of Contents

Introduction	v
Part One: The Myth	**1**
Offending Venus	3
The Labours	5
Immortality and the Birth of Pleasure	16
Venus and Cupid: our Allies on the Road to Wholeness	17
Psyche: A Modern Venusian Revolution	21
Summary	27
Part Two: When the Progressed Sun Shines on Psyche	**29**
Introduction	31
Simone de Beauvoir	33
Friedrich Nietzsche	39
John Lennon	44
Camille	50
Madame du Châtelet	53
Isaac Newton	58
Gérard de Nerval	61
Marie-Antoinette	66
Maria Montessori	72
Jeanne	77
Marcel Proust	79
Robert Francis Kennedy	85
The Connection Between the Asteroid, the Myth and Projection	92
Part Three: The Astrological Psyche	**95**
Psyche in the Birth Chart	97
When Psyche Causes Suffering	107
Psyche in Transit	108
Transits and progressions to Psyche	115

Part Four: Psyche in Aspect — **117**
   Psyche in Aspect to the Sun — 119
   Psyche in Aspect to the Moon — 146
   Some thoughts on Moon-Psyche aspects — 161
   The Fathers and Mothers of Psychoanalysis – Psyche and Jupiter, Saturn, and Pluto — 163
   Psyche in Cross-Aspects: Thoughts on Synastry — 167

Conclusion — **179**

Bibliography — 181

About the Author — 184

Introduction

Psyche was the sixteenth asteroid to be discovered, in 1852. Her name comes from the Greek ψυχή, *psukhê*, the breath that animates the body, i.e. the soul. Her symbol represents a butterfly wing surmounted by a star. She orbits the Sun in the asteroid belt, located between Mars and Jupiter. Psyche is three times further from the Sun than the Earth is. Her surface area is roughly equivalent to that of New Zealand or Indonesia, which qualifies her as a giant asteroid. A NASA mission is currently underway to determine the asteroid's composition, and in particular the metal content, which is thought to be quite high, accounting for 30–60% of its volume. Launched in 2023, it won't start providing answers until 2029. Psyche takes about five years to circle the Sun, with a slightly elliptical orbit. She spends a variable amount of time in each sign of the zodiac, ranging from two to ten months (when she turns retrograde).

Part One

The Myth

The earliest written version of the Psyche myth was handed down to us by Apuleius in the second century CE.[1] Apuleius was born in North Africa into a relatively well-off, Romanised Berber family. He studied rhetoric in Carthage, then went to Athens to study philosophy, particularly Platonic. In Greece, he was initiated into mysteries and secret cults. The myth of Psyche predates Apuleius, but he adapted it to his own culture and philosophy. Many elements of the myth refer to Libyan culture (the ant, the reed, the tower), and similarly structured Kabyle tales have been identified – Apuleius had taken a Libyan oral tradition and Romanised it.

---

1 Lucius Apuleius, *The Golden Ass*, trans. E. J. Kenney (Penguin Classics, 1999).

Offending Venus

The myth begins by discussing the harm that a king's daughter, Psyche, inflicts on the cult of Venus through her beauty alone: "her rites were abandoned, her temples disfigured, her couches trampled, her worship neglected; her statues were ungarlanded, her altars shamefully cold." The supreme sacrilege: it's the mortal before whom people kneel; it's her they invoke from now on. Venus must take revenge for this affront. First, she tries to use her son Cupid to achieve her ends: she demands that Psyche fall in love with the "lowest of mankind", a wretch without rank or fortune. The need for Psyche to marry "something cruel and fierce and serpentine" is announced to her father by the oracle of Apollo of Miletus. Psyche submits and obeys the divine sentence, but not without asking her parents to stop crying, for "Then, when nations and peoples were paying us divine honours, when with one voice they were hailing me as a new Venus, then you should have grieved [...] now I see that it is by the name of Venus alone that I am destroyed." Apuleius insists: it's indeed Venus, dishonoured, who takes her revenge.

But Cupid, disobeying his mother, chooses to prick himself with his arrow in the presence of Psyche, in order to fall in love with her and make her his wife. Having installed her in his palace, where she enjoys the utmost luxury, he visits her every night, making it a condition of this life of pleasure that she never try to discover who he is. Psyche accepts this meaningless but comfortable and secure existence. She shares her bed with a man she neither knows nor has chosen, and has thus symbolically renounced all forms of self-expression. She then learns from her mysterious husband that she's carrying a child, who will be a god if she keeps silent, but a mortal if she reveals their secret. Psyche's sisters, horribly jealous of her happiness and especially of her wealth, succeed in persuading her that her husband really is the monster of prophecy, and she must prepare to kill him while he sleeps, by setting him alight with an oil lamp.

The myth shifts at this point, at the moment of unveiling; as we shall see later, the encounter with the asteroid Psyche is always associated with a moment of revealing. By illuminating Cupid, she gains access to the beauty of the divine: "as she gazed and gazed on the beauty of the god's face, her spirits returned." As if hypnotised, she mechanically touches the god's arrows, "Thus unknowingly Psyche through her own act fell in love with Love." This sentence tells us that Psyche wasn't in love with her husband before this scene of unveiling. Many interpretations of this myth speak of a breach of trust, of doubt leading to the loss of the beloved, as Cupid flees as soon as he knows he has been recognised. But it appears that true love is born at the moment of unveiling, the precise moment when Psyche sees who her husband really is, which gives a very different interpretation of the myth, leaving aside the story of betrayed trust.

The Labours

Love according to Plato

To understand and interpret what follows, namely the labours imposed by Venus, I'll refer to two frameworks: astrological symbolism and Platonic philosophy. Plato, a disciple of Socrates, portrayed the latter in numerous works. One of them, *The Symposium* (which, in its French version, is subtitled "about love"), must be considered if we're to understand the myth of Psyche, for it evokes both Aphrodite and Cupid. What's more, Apuleius, who wrote of this myth, also wrote a work entitled *De Platone*: so he was a connoisseur of the master's philosophy. In *The Symposium*, philosophers take turns to praise love, each from their own point of view. Socrates ends his account of an encounter with a wise, foreign woman, Diotime, by expressing his views on immortality: "Such [...] were the words of Diotima; and I am persuaded of their truth. And being persuaded of them, I try to persuade others that in the attainment of this end [immortality] human nature will not easily find a helper better than love."[2] As the myth ends with the union between Cupid and Psyche, the latter becoming immortal thanks to her love for Cupid, it's hard not to see a reference to Socrates and Plato. As we shall see, to achieve true love and immortality, Psyche must perform four labours that reflect the Platonic virtues of wisdom, temperance or moderation, courage and justice.

Longing is the fuel for the quest

Psyche, with her oil lamp, has seen Cupid, felt "reborn" and fallen "in love with Love." She's no longer the passive woman waiting for a husband she doesn't even know, bored to death in her palace, but a woman in love who knows the one her heart has chosen, a choice symbolised by the fact she pricks herself with the arrows. But as soon as she falls in love with Cupid,

---

[2] Plato, *The Symposium* (Penguin Classics; Reissue edition 2003).

she loses him: awakened by hot oil dripping from the lamp, Cupid is burnt and flees. So Psyche loses the object of her desire as soon as she falls in love with him. This isn't surprising, if we refer to Socrates's demonstration in *The Symposium*: "And the admission has been already made that Eros is [desire] of something which a man wants and has not." Psyche must by necessity lose Cupid in order to desire him, and it's this desire that will cause her to endure the punishments Venus will inflict upon her. We shall see that loss and longing are at the heart of the astrological interpretation of the asteroid Psyche.

Goddesses who refuse help

Psyche seeks the help of two goddesses, Ceres and Juno, but they refuse her, for fear of alienating Venus, who is looking for the woman who dared to burn her son. These two goddesses – Demeter and Hera to the Greeks – possess a lunar dimension. Demeter is the mother of Kore, who will become Persephone, and she's the goddess who feeds humans. The symbolism of food and the mother-child bond belongs to the lunar, not the Venusian, world. Hera is the goddess of family and marriage, protecting the institution and the security offered by the family clan. These two lunar goddesses evolve in a different world from Venus, who has no morals and thinks only of herself. If Venus protects emotional ties, it's insofar as they are a source of pleasure and joy, and not in the name of duty or social respectability. Demeter and Hera can do nothing to help Psyche appease the fury of an outraged Venus, and the young mortal eventually gives in and submits to the goddess. Venus first has her tortured by her servants Care and Sorrow *(Sollicitudo atque Tristities)*. Their names illustrate not only what the loss of a loved one can bring, but also, astrologically speaking, what's likely to happen to us when we fail to honour the goddess Venus within us. We'll see that anxiety or sadness can be experienced when we encounter the asteroid Psyche. After having Psyche tortured, Venus imposes four labours on her, which reflect the qualities we must develop to be ready to honour her. These qualities are the four cardinal virtues of the Platonists, but they also have astrological symbolism.

First labour

Psyche must first sort through a gigantic pile of seven different kinds of seeds. As she despairs, an ant emerges to do the job with the help of its colony. This first task illustrates the Platonic virtue of wisdom, which consists in exercising one's capacity for discernment, or, more generally, one's reason. One of Solomon's proverbs from the Old Testament, which predates Apuleius's writing of the myth, states: "Go to the ant, thou sluggard; consider her ways, and be wise." Many Greek authors (including Hesiod, Aristotle and Plato) mention ants for their wisdom and intelligence.

The number of different seeds, seven, is no coincidence in a myth in which Apuleius is trying hard to get a message across. Seven is a number associated with the Divine for the Pythagoreans, as Apuleius reminds us at the end of *the Golden Ass/Metamorphoses* (the work in which the myth of Psyche and Cupid appears); the seeds are mixed together, they are indistinguishable in this immense heap, and there are no longer any boundaries between the different types. In sorting out these seeds, Psyche is invited to be discriminating and to avoid confusion. Bearing in mind that it's Venus who decides what work Psyche must do, we can deduce that in order to establish a healthy relationship with Cupid, Psyche must learn to set limits, to avoid melting into the other, to avoid the Neptunian temptation to become one with the beloved. Seven is also the number of celestial bodies visible in the sky and known at the time: the Sun, the Moon, Mercury, Venus, Mars, Jupiter and Saturn. Again, it's important to distinguish the function and domain of each planet, so each can play their own role. Lunar needs, for example, mustn't prevent us from establishing Venusian-type relationships, in which our values are central, by making us prefer secure relationships, which could keep us in a state of dependence. If the Sun urges us to find meaning in our lives, it can't do so without Venus, without whom our lives would be devoid of joy and self-esteem. Having recourse to Mars and his assertiveness shouldn't prevent us from aspiring to a certain harmony, and using Mercury to understand the world, or ourselves, mustn't be to the detriment of what Venus represents, particularly in her emotional and bodily dimension.

Helped by the ant, Psyche uses her discernment to identify each seed. Honouring Venus means above all making choices, knowing how to sort out what's authentic to us and what doesn't belong to us, what we value (what we find beautiful) and what doesn't concern us. The myth of the Judgement of Paris illustrates the intrinsic link between choice and Venus, as the young prince chooses Aphrodite. In astrological terms, Venus is intimately linked to our values. The choice of the person with whom we establish a Venusian relationship, Apuleius reminds us, can't be made without wisdom, that is, without discernment. We must value this person because they correspond with our values, otherwise the relationship will be meaningless.

We're used to thinking of Libra, ruled by Venus, as the sign where interpersonal relationships begin. The self is built in the first six signs, then we're invited to establish relationships, particularly romantic ones, in Libra and Scorpio, and finally, to take the risk of social involvement from Sagittarius onwards. And yet, the astrological sign that best illustrates this initial Psychean work is Virgo: for the meticulousness of the work to be done, on the one hand, and for the notion of sorting. This sign is a fundamental step towards the world of interpersonal relationships, which symbolically begins with Libra. Thanks to its discernment and wisdom, Virgo enables us to establish boundaries with others. Virgo doesn't belong to anyone, doesn't merge with anyone, and isn't for sale: this sign will build relationships based on its own values, always favouring inner integrity. Many people distance themselves from Venus, basing their choices not on their own values, but on what will make them feel appropriate or acceptable to the group. Others have no idea what they find beautiful, what gives them pleasure or what their values are. Psyche has to sort out the seeds, showing us that this work of finding what we value has to be done beforehand, as Venus demands. Still others lose their sense of personal worth by leaving it in the hands of others: they value themselves only when they're loved and enter a spiral of emotional dependence. Again, Virgo isn't for sale, and isn't dependent on anyone: Virgo is therefore well suited to honouring Venus, even though this is traditionally the sign of her fall. But the opposite sign, that of her exaltation, Pisces, may lack this virginal discernment, and if love is granted to everyone, or unconditionally, Venus risks being overshadowed by Neptune. The qualities of Virgo make it possible to love, admire or appreciate, while remaining true to oneself, because the person has been chosen according to inner and authentic criteria.

Second labour

The second task consists in bringing Venus a flake of wool from sheep whose fleece is golden. A reed explains to Psyche that the Sun, imparting its warmth to them, stirs them to a fierce rage that drives them to attack humans to the death. These golden sheep, excited by the Sun, evoke the myth of Jason and the Golden Fleece, the sign of Aries and the exaltation of the Sun in this sign. According to the reed, for Psyche to succeed in her labour she must resist the characteristic rashness of the first sign and wait until "the midday heat of the sun abates and the flock is quietened." Noon evokes the sign of Leo, ruled by the Sun. What's more, in the region of Africa where Apuleius came from, there are traces of myths about heliophoric rams, which were therefore solar symbols. The cardinal virtue emphasised in this work is temperance or moderation, because Psyche isn't authorised to act immediately. She can only gather a flake of this golden (solar) fleece if she waits until the heat of the star has dissipated, which means she must be wary of both the signs of Leo and Aries.

Venus is certainly at the service of the Sun, the core of the individual, but she can only play her role as its ally if the person doesn't remain focused on personal flowering, as evoked by the sign of Leo: we must take the risk of entering into relationships, which traditionally begin in Libra but whose foundations are in Virgo – as seen earlier, establishing healthy boundaries and making choices are essential prerequisites. This work is also a reminder that Venus is in exile in Aries. The impatience and impetuosity of the first sign, and Aries's desire to get going again, to move forward, taking the risk of leaving something satisfying behind, don't suit Venus who encourages us to stay in a relationship as long as it's a source of pleasure.

For Plato and Apuleius, temperance is also a way of ensuring that carnal passions, which Apuleius called "the fruit of shameful pleasures", or our "desires and appetites" don't get the better of the first virtue, wisdom. While Venus-Taurus invites us not to ignore our senses when it comes to honouring the goddess, self-realisation in relationships requires discernment and moderation. Physical pleasure is one of the components of self-esteem and self-love Venus offers, but she requires us to choose, according to our values, the person with whom we experience it.

Leo and Aries were chosen by Apuleius because the fire that animates them can be synonymous with passions and desires, which, when out of control, can bite us "with their venomous teeth" like the sheep in the myth. Since Plato refers to moderation as the virtue that balances desires and appetites, we can understand why Apuleius chose the image of sheep, covered in gold and excited by the Sun, which refers to both Leo and Aries. As Apuleius explains: "Look at the wise man: the prospect of pleasure, however lively it may be, will not induce him to act unless it's accompanied by honourable profits."[3] Venus can only have a golden flake, and be the Sun's ally, if Psyche knows how to contain, thanks to her temperance, the heat of the Sun exalted in Aries and the desires of Mars its ruler, in order to act with wisdom acquired during the previous labour.

Third labour

"Now however I am going to put myself out to discover if your heart is really stout and your prudence unequalled." With these words, Venus shows she has understood that Psyche is capable of virtue (prudence being synonymous with wisdom in Plato). Now she is about to test her courage (her heart).

In the third labour, Psyche is confronted with icy black waters protected by dragons, from which she must fill a bottle for Venus. It's an eagle, the regal bird of Jupiter, who will save her from the worst, leaving "Jove's pathways in the heights", dodging the dragons and persuading the waters to let him approach on the pretext that he needs water for Venus's bath. Here we have two symbols to question: the ice-cold black waters and the eagle. In astrology, the three water signs, Cancer, Scorpio and Pisces, are cold-blooded animals. Representing the function Jung calls "feeling", they relate to the world of emotions, which is deep, opaque and black, as opposed to the symbolism of the air signs, which are humans (the twins and the water bearer) or an object (the scales).

Psyche is therefore challenged in this third Venusian work to allow Venus to bathe in emotions. But the emotional world is dangerous: it's guarded by dragons, which symbolise the defences we erect to protect ourselves from what we feel. Air signs, in particular, are likely to be wary of their feelings, and they may choose their love partner rationally and logically, based on ideological criteria, when, of course, the heart has its

---

3   Lucius Apuleius, *De Platone et eius dogmate* (Createspace Independent Publishing Platform, 2014).

reasons that reason ignores. Venus-ruled Libra, the sign of the zodiac that symbolically marks the beginning of the ability to form partnerships, is an air sign, but Venus needs to bathe in water – to confront the emotional realm. Each water sign has a different way of looking at and dealing with emotions, but what all three have in common is that they attach great importance to them in love relationships or even friendship. Deep waters are particularly evocative of Scorpio, as are dragons, which belong to the snake group – the animal that used to symbolise this constellation before Scorpio was chosen. This sign has mastery over the dark, icy waters of emotions, especially those that would otherwise be suppressed.

Let's now look at the second symbol, the eagle. The eagle was a very important animal in ancient times: Aquila (the term used in the Latin version) is Zeus's thunderbolt carrier. In Apuleius's time, the eagle was the emblem of the Roman legion, and represented Roman strength, power and courage. Psyche has already been warned in the previous work: she's not expected to express Martian aggressiveness. But the courage to choose is an essential quality if we're to honour Venus and avoid her vengeance. We've seen how the notion of choice is at the heart of the expression of Venus, but if it requires wisdom, it often requires courage as well. In choosing Aphrodite, the young Trojan Paris alienates the powerful Hera and Athena, who in this context can embody a form of submission to the established order, to family (Hera) and to reason (Athena). Honouring Venus sometimes requires us to alienate people whose judgement condemns us, or to leave relationships that have ceased to be a source of joy in order to establish new ones. Finally, building an authentic relationship requires a different kind of courage: the courage to face our emotions, to face what may be unconscious in us, represented here by the dark waters.

This passage with the eagle is an illustration of the virtue of courage. Apuleius makes it clear the eagle is leaving Jove's pathways. Jupiter rules the sign that follows Scorpio, Sagittarius. Like the air signs, this sign can flee the emotional world by taking refuge in the world of the mind, of symbols, and in belonging to a social group rather than a duo in which emotional ties are central. But it can also find the courage to confront the unconscious and the emotions, if it consents to leave Jupiterian spaces, the reassuring spaces of the mind, spirituality or philosophical detachment, and retain only the eagle's courage and piercing vision. Generally speaking, the other fire signs, while less inclined to inner questioning, also possess the courage to confront difficulties.

Psyche is on the verge of failure: Apuleius writes that she remains petrified when she sees the impossibility of her task and "though her body was present her senses were elsewhere." In *De Platone*, he explains that the opposite of courage is insensitivity, so courage is about to fail the princess. Psyche needs help. Thus, armed with his courage, legendary in the Roman world, and his exceptional vision, the Eagle seconds her and confronts the emotional world. He allows Venus to bathe in feelings, she who, in Taurus, is at ease with the sensual aspect of relationships, and in Libra, with the ideals of equality, justice and rationality. So Venus isn't naturally comfortable in water signs, and this is why this work requires courage. Venus is exalted in Pisces, but it's the love of the divine or universal love that's honoured; in Cancer, it can be difficult to express Venus because we're in lunar territory, and in Scorpio, Venus is in exile. But Aquila, the eagle with the piercing eye, knows Venus must bathe in the waters of the emotions if the union is to contribute towards the solar expression of the individual.

Fourth labour

Psyche's final task is her descent into Hades's realm, to bring back to Venus "a little of [Proserpine]'s beauty." The fact that Psyche is to meet the ruler of the Underworld establishes an unnatural link between Venus and the sign of Scorpio. Entering the world of the dead indicates Psyche is ready to undergo her metamorphosis, which requires a new birth and therefore a previous death. We now know that Pluto, the Roman equivalent of Hades, is the planet that presides over a similar process. Although Pluto was unknown to the ancients, the sign he rules, Scorpio, was associated with death and resurrection, since the feasts of Osiris were celebrated in Egypt during the month of Khoiak, with celebrations ending on 15 November. We can therefore recall the symbolism of this sign to help us understand this last work of Psyche. Venus rules Taurus and is therefore in exile in Scorpio. Yet Venus wants a little of the beauty of Proserpine. How can the goddess of beauty need someone else's beauty? The beauty of Scorpio, the beauty of Proserpine, is buried deep and resides in a realm where neither Venus-Taurus nor Venus-Libra would seem to belong. If Taurus can enjoy daily life together in the simplicity of being with the other person or by sharing sensual pleasures, Scorpio will look for something in the relationship that relates to the truth of being, to the deep communion of souls. While Libra would like to pretend we have no shadows and our behaviour in a relationship is fair and guided by reason, Scorpio knows from childhood that this isn't the case. Projections, especially those related to early relationships with parents, make people irrational, and the unconscious fear of being submissive to the other person can create power struggles that don't speak their name. Venus is certainly in exile in Scorpio, losing the innocence and comfort she'd have in Taurus. But she gains depth and truth, and thanks to the work done in Scorpio, Venus can make intense soul-to-soul connections.

In his work, Apuleius addresses the fourth Platonic virtue, that of justice. To understand this, we need to look at what Psyche has to do during this journey. Advised by a tower from which she was planning to commit suicide, she must keep two obols (ancient Greek coin) in her mouth to give to Charon so she can cross the River Styx on the way there and on the way back. She must also have cakes of barley meal in each of her hands to feed Cerberus on her arrival and departure. When she arrives at Proserpine's palace, she must refuse to sit comfortably and eat with pleasure, telling the goddess that she prefers to sit on the floor and eat *panem sordidum* (*panis sordidus* in Rome was bread for dogs made exclusively from bran). Finally, so as not to lose her cakes, Psyche must refrain from helping anyone along her way, even though a lame donkey driver, a dead old man and three weavers will successively ask for her help. All these details evoke the fourth virtue: justice. According to Plato, justice corresponds to the desire to give everyone their due, and to do only what falls within one's role. The obols to Charon, the food to Cerberus; to Psyche, a mere mortal, neither the seats nor the food of the gods, but those of the animals. And to the donkey-driver, the old man and the weavers, who implore her and try to pity her: nothing. Everyone gets their due.

According to Apuleius, in *De Platone*, an individual is "just" when each part of their soul performs its functions without interfering with those of other elements; he points out that Plato considered wisdom to be the ruler of the soul ($\psi\upsilon\chi\acute{\eta}$), with courage and temperance at its service. Thus, while showing that Psyche plays her own role well (she takes the *panis sordidum* and sits on the ground), and gives Cerberus and Charon what she owes them, he reminds us of the extent to which she now demonstrates the other three virtues, while letting wisdom reign supreme. In this work, Psyche needed courage to dare to descend into the Underworld, and moderation to resist her instinct to help those who asked for her help. Indeed, Apuleius, in *De Platone*, considered giving without moderation to be a vice, for entire estates are wiped out "by its excessive profligacy." Wisdom retained its role as primary guide, making Psyche listen to and follow the advice of the tower.

On the Venusian plane, justice reminds us that wisdom remains our best ally in a relationship: as seen earlier, it consists of making choices based on our values. What's more, like Psyche, who refuses to elevate herself to the level of a goddess or to give people who ask for her help what isn't their due, a healthy expression of Venus requires us to take our own role to heart, that is, to remain within the framework of our unique essence, of which the birth chart is a reflection. It's well known that one of the risks for the lover is to play a role in order to conform to the other person's desires. The lover can also fall into the opposite trap, demanding that the other person play a role in order to please them. Finally, the lover must be careful not to put themselves at the service of the person they love, i.e. to give them more than they deserve, thus deviating from their own path. If Psyche helps the old man or the weavers, she'll remain a prisoner in the Underworld, for she will lose her obols to Charon or her cakes to Cerberus. To be just in the Platonic sense requires a kind of descent into Hades, for we can't be truly just if we haven't dared to face the unconscious. It's the process of individuation in the Jungian sense: a process that enables us to find the role we want to play, the one that really suits us. Becoming oneself requires access to the unconscious and presupposes that we're able to remain ourselves in a relationship, without being just one half of a couple, without playing the role projected onto us.

Finally, Psyche seems to have succeeded in her mission in every respect. However, the tower had warned her: the most important piece of advice it gave her was to not open the bottle, because what it contained belonged to a divinity. If Psyche continues to follow the Platonic virtues, in particular that of justice, she shouldn't open the bottle containing Proserpine's beauty and intended for Venus. But out of curiosity, and to seduce her lover, she does so. All she finds is "an infernal sleep" and she falls, nothing more than a "sleeping corpse." Did Psyche stumble on the last step of her Venusian labour? For the second time, she is curious, and for the second time, drama ensues, hence the hasty interpretation we too often read, according to which Psyche is a tale of trust betrayed in a love relationship. On the contrary, twice, Psyche's curiosity brings her face to face with the divine: thanks to her lamp, she contemplates the divine beauty of Cupid; opening the bottle, she wishes to obtain the beauty of a goddess, to be worthy of that of her lover.

The sleep that falls upon Psyche isn't a punishment, although it's described as "infernal". Following the Platonic idea of the initiatory path, with beauty as its guide, which I'll explore in greater detail later, this sleep is a kind of chrysalis in which the soul completes its metamorphosis. It's ready for this transformation when, having contemplated the beauty of the divine, having endeavoured to regain it by showing itself to be virtuous, it dares to want to appropriate it. That's what Psyche did by trying to make Proserpine's beauty her own. Proserpine, better than anyone, knows it may be necessary to die to become oneself; she who was Kore and who, torn from her mother and forced to enter the kingdom of Hades, became its sovereign. Psyche too will change her identity and kingdom to live on Olympus. Indeed, Cupid is there to save her: he can rid her of the torpor that surrounds her, awaken her by gently pricking her with his arrow, and ask his father Jupiter for her immortality.

Immortality and the Birth of Pleasure

The sacred marriage

If we follow a Platonic interpretation, Psyche has shown she can develop the four cardinal virtues: the soul is therefore virtuous and desirous of divine beauty, and is now worthy of immortality. Jupiter agrees to his son's request and makes Psyche drink the divine nectar, then declares the union of Psyche and Cupid "legitimate and in accordance with the civil law." These words from the king of the gods are important, as they mark respect for the law in the union between Psyche and Cupid: a god can only marry an immortal. It is of course a reference to the exaltation of Saturn, the law, in Libra, where Venus is ruler. This notion of equality in the relationship, with each party recognising the other's status as subject, is crucial to any understanding of the asteroid, since it refers to the virtue of justice. The myth ends with Psyche's immortality and Venus's joy: now nothing but sweetness, she dances at her son's wedding feast. The gift of Venus to Psyche, in imposing her labours on her, is therefore the revelation of her divine beauty, which gives her equality in her relationship with Cupid and immortality.

Well-deserved pleasure

But these are not the only gifts Psyche receives: she is now ready to give birth to her child, symbolically to give form to what was still only a potential. This child was given the name of Pleasure – *Voluptas* in Latin. *Voluptas* means pleasure, joy, satisfaction and contentment. Apuleius grants Psyche and Cupid the right to pleasure and joy in their marriage, but they were only able to achieve this because Psyche succeeded in developing the virtues described in the myth. These qualities are therefore essential to achieve a union that's not only happy, but also egalitarian and part of one's sense of achievement, as symbolised by ultimate immortality. We will see that these qualities are symbolised by the sign, house and aspects of the asteroid Psyche in our chart.

Venus and Cupid: our Allies on the Road to Wholeness

The two deities at the centre of the myth are Venus and her son Cupid. To understand the significance of the asteroid Psyche in the birth chart, it's useful to look back at some of their dimensions in ancient Greece.

The two Venuses

Venus, goddess of beauty and love, isn't at the centre of the Psyche myth by chance. Reading Apuleius's *Apologia*, his defence against accusations of using magic, gives an idea of what he thought of the goddess. He explains he's been initiated into the mysteries of Plato's school, and that he'd say nothing about them, with the exception of one example linked to Venus. According to the secret teachings he'd received, there are two Venuses. One rules over men and animals and infuses them with vulgar desires and physical passions. The other, the celestial Venus, makes us choose the person of our heart according to the nobility of their soul, whose beauty reminds us of the divine beauty we saw before our soul was incarnated in our body. Apuleius certainly doesn't say everything he knows. He's merely recalling what's already said in Plato's *Symposium*, when Pausanias states there's an ancient, motherless Aphrodite, daughter of Ouranos, called celestial (Ourania) and a younger Aphrodite, daughter of Zeus and Dionè, called popular (*Pandèmos*). The rest of Pausanias's speech may be surprising, as he explains that the celestial Aphrodite encourages men to love boys and shun women. But we need to think beyond questions of homo- or heterosexuality. Aphrodite Pandèmos attracts us to those who are dissimilar to us, because it's with them that we can reproduce, and as such she concerns human beings as much as animals. She ensures the survival of a species, and thus concerns necessity. Aphrodite Ourania, born without a mother and therefore symbolically unattached to matter and belonging to the realm of the spirit, urges us towards a person who resembles us, but not just any person: one who possesses a share of the divine beauty that's also ours. In this way, through Eros, this goddess instils in us a love for the qualities within us that we'll develop and reveal by falling in love with a similar beauty in another human being. This is where the other becomes our mirror, the famous mirror that Aphrodite always has in her hand, because they reflect a part of us whose expression is necessary for wholeness and the expression of our individuality, our solar qualities.

Venus, the Sun's ally

Having emphasised the links between Venus and the Sun in the previous paragraphs, it may be useful to recall the mythological and astrological links between them. In Greek mythology, Hesiod calls her "Golden Aphrodite" and describes her as "smiling". Homer, in the *Iliad*, uses the same two epithets, "golden" and "smiling". Gold refers to solar qualities, and a smile to joy. Aphrodite is the guarantor of authentic joy, as she allows solar qualities to express themselves. In the "Judgment of Paris", Aphrodite gets the golden apple. Hephaestus, her husband, melts the gold to make her finery and the golden bed in which he attaches her, with golden ties, to her lover Ares, to expose them to the judgment of the other gods and goddesses.

In the myth of Psyche, Venus is particularly cruel. She's also cruel in the myth of the Minotaur, since she's responsible for the unnatural love between Minos's wife Pasiphae and a bull. She also provoked the Trojan War by offering the wife of a Greek king to a Trojan prince. Greek mythology is full of her tantrums and revenges. This teaches us that if Venus doesn't find her rightful place in our lives, she will take revenge and make us suffer. She can inflict destructive passion, as well as an inner emptiness akin to depression, if we choose to ignore her.

Venus, to bring us closer to the Sun and help us discover who we are, does travel the roads of Taurus and Libra: but these are means, not ends. The objects that arouse our desire, and the relationships that inflame us, aren't the goals pursued by Venus: they're merely means of defining ourselves, the famous Venusian mirrors. The object of our desire is a support for the projection of what's precious and golden in us, what allows us to live our solar qualities. She demands that we define our values, make our choices, and stay true to them in order to feel a genuine sense of self-esteem and of self-worth. As Venus is traditionally known as the planet of love, honouring Venus is truly about self-love.

At the end of the myth, "Apollo sang to the lyre, and Venus, fitting her steps to the sweet music, danced in all her beauty." Venus fits her step to Apollo's music: the goddess is finally in her role as ally of the Sun, since she has enabled the soul to find its divine beauty. Through her labours, she has given Psyche the opportunity to experience her solar immortality, the profound meaning of her own life.

Venus and the mysteries of love

Apuleius considers the love of beauty to be a path of initiation for the soul, with Venus as a guide. In this, he follows a Platonic tradition. Some astrologers have developed similar visions of Venus, such as Dane Rudhyar, who sees her as the Alchemist and Initiator, the one who opens the gate to the transcendental mind-realms, to the Universals.[4] In his view, Venus represents the alchemical process of extracting the spiritual from the material, the alchemical gold being the purest love as well as the purest sensation, i.e. the aesthetic sensation that enables us to perceive beauty.

In *the Symposium*, Diotime explains to Socrates how love can lead to salvation through beauty: "These are the lesser mysteries of love, into which even you, Socrates, may enter; to the greater and more hidden ones which are the crown of these, and to which, if you pursue them in a right spirit, they will lead, I know not whether you will be able to attain." First, love the beauty of a single body, then all beautiful bodies, then love the beauty of souls, then the beauty that lies in actions and laws, that which lies in knowledge, and finally absolute, eternal, i.e., divine Beauty, that which belongs to no object, no person, no idea. By contemplating absolute Beauty, the soul can't but desire virtue, and in so doing, it becomes cherished by God and deserves immortality. Socrates concludes his account of Diotime's words by saying she's convinced him that our best ally in this world, in attaining the divine and immortality, is love. Psyche, then, is an illustration of what becomes possible when one follows the Venusian initiation (the labours): the attainment of bliss and immortality.

---

4 Dane Rudhyar, *New Mansions for New Men* (Borodino Books 2017).

Cupid, the torch-carrier

These "mysteries of love" are also related to the divine within us, which is reached through the individuation process, as introduced by Jung, of which love is an extremely powerful driving force. This force, this energy, is symbolised by Venus's son, Cupid – Eros in Greek. In Greco-Roman antiquity, Cupid was seen as an enlightener. He was sometimes depicted with a torch, sometimes burning a butterfly's wing. The latter, symbol of the soul (and of the asteroid Psyche), goes through a process of purification by fire, in the image of the alchemical *calcinatio*, so the soul can gain access to something authentic and deeply buried. Among other epithets, Eros was known as the "purifier of the soul". In her work on the interpretation of the *Golden Ass* (also known as *The Metamorphoses*, and in which the myth of Psyche is found), Marie-Louise von Franz quotes a prayer to Eros in which he is invoked in the following terms: "You engender an unseen fire / as you carry off every living thing without growing weary of torturing it, rather having with pleasure delighted in pain from the time when the world came into being. [...] archer, torch-carrier, master of all living/sensation and of everything clandestine, dispenser of forgetfulness, creator of silence, through whom the light and to whom the light travels." [5] [6] When we fall in love, Eros lights us up with his torch, burns us with his fire and shows the goal with his arrow. Psyche, the asteroid in our chart, can only be activated during transits and progressions if Eros has already brought us into contact with someone we love. We shall see that these are love relationships in the truest sense of the word (Beauvoir-Sartre) as well as relationships we'd describe as friendly, but which can drive us just as much, when they seem vital to us (Lennon-McCartney, Wagner-Nietzsche).

---

5   Marie-Louise von Franz, *The Golden Ass of Apuleius: The Liberation of the Feminine in Man* (C. G. Jung Foundation Books Series, 2001).
6   K. Preisendanz. *The Greek Magical Papyri in Translation Including the Demotic Spells*. PGM IV. 1716-1870 p.70.

Psyche: A Modern Venusian Revolution

True love according to Plato: Lucius and Isis

The myth of Psyche and Cupid is part of *The Golden Ass* (or *The Metamorphoses*), which recounts the life of Lucius (whose first name is the same as that of Apuleius). He's transformed into a donkey because, with the help of his mistress, he tried to use magic without knowing or mastering it. He recounts his adventures, which begin when he is stolen by robbers to be used as a pack animal. When the same brigands kidnap a young woman called Charitè for ransom, Lucius overhears the old woman who accompanies the brigands telling her the myth of Psyche and Cupid to distract her from her grief.

After many adventures, Lucius is awakened one night by a flash of light: it's a full moon. Remembering that "the Moon-goddess, sole sovereign of mankind [...] is the shining deity by whose divine influence not only all beasts, wild and tame, but all inanimate things as well, are invigorated", he makes an appeal to the lunar divinity, whom he calls Ceres, celestial Venus, Artemis and Proserpine. Then Isis appears to him, her black cloak decorated with stars and a full, fiery moon. She tells him she has been given many different names, including Diana, Hecate, Dictynna, Aphrodite, Proserpine and Juno, but explains that only the Ethiopians and the Egyptians call her by her real name, Queen Isis.

Isis gives him back his human appearance, and Lucius, amazed, wants to be initiated into her mysteries, but he hesitates because of the obligation to respect the vow of chastity. In the end, he joyfully accepts his initiation. He explains that "the rites of initiation approximate to a voluntary death from which there is only a precarious hope of resurrection" and recounts the great day in these words: "I approached the very gates of death and set one foot on Proserpine's threshold, yet was permitted to return." After this initiation, which preceded a second, this time into the mysteries of Osiris,

Lucius ends his life in the service of these divinities, in the bliss of a chaste love of the divine, as Socrates describes in Plato's *Symposium*.

Apuleius and the Third Species of Love

Lucius was on the verge of death, reminiscent of what happens to Psyche in the realm of Proserpine, except Lucius knew what was coming and fully accepted it. But this apparent death is the final stage of a metamorphosis that makes love worthy, reminiscent of the metamorphosis of the caterpillar into the butterfly, symbol of the asteroid and the soul.

But Psyche is not Lucius, because Apuleius, aware that the purity of love that Lucius vows to the divine is accessible only to a small number of his fellow men and women, and wishing above all to spare them the other type of love, content with physical pleasure, opens a third path, which he'd already presented in *De Platone*: "There is also a third species of love, which we have denominated a medium, and which subsists through an affinity to divine and terrestrial love, is connected to each by an equal bond of alliance, and in the same manner as divine love is proximate to reason, and is joined to the desire of pleasure, like the terrestrial love."

Thanks to her efforts, Psyche can reach this third kind of love, divine and earthly at the same time: she will live on Mount Olympus and be immortal, but she'll be equal to her husband and will give birth to a daughter called Pleasure. This sensuality has nothing to do with the "most filthy, brutal, and base love" that feeds only on the pleasures of the body.[7] Apuleius has clearly demonstrated that Psyche has shown herself to be worthy and virtuous, and Cupid himself (this is beyond the scope of this book) has also evolved through trials to fall in love with Psyche's soul and not just her body. Apuleius thus explores the ways of human love and recognises its dignity, even if Lucius's revelation shows that the most perfect love is that dedicated to the primordial goddess.

For Apuleius, divine and earthly love are attainable by a human being if they show themselves capable of achieving what Psyche has achieved: they must show discernment, making choices and avoiding fusion with the beloved (first labour), show moderation, avoiding acting according to their senses (second labour), develop courage to stand by their values and go and

---

7   Lucius Apuleius, *De Platone et eius dogmate* (Createspace Independent Publishing Platform, 2014).

confront the unconscious and their buried emotions (third labour), and finally be able to stay true to themself in the relationship and not play a role someone else wants them to play (fourth labour). Whenever the asteroid Psyche is activated by transiting or progressed planets in the natal chart, these themes are updated. Venus can be honoured under these conditions, favouring a happy union ("Pleasure") between two equal beings ("in accordance with the civil law"). She will then favour the person's Sun, giving them access to their symbolic immortality.

The Discovery of Psyche and Romanticism

Psyche was the sixteenth asteroid to be discovered, on 17 March 1852. On that day the Sun was in Pisces, the sign of exaltation of Venus, who was in Taurus, the sign she rules. The Sun formed a very close quincunx with the asteroid Psyche, which was in Leo. It's striking that Psyche was right on Regulus at this time, as if her reign was ready to come. But what really deserves our attention are the aspects Venus formed with the other planets of the chart. If we were dealing with a person, we'd describe these aspects as particularly difficult. Venus was in conjunction to Pluto, Saturn and Uranus, the latter two planets being in the same degree of the zodiac, in other words in very close conjunction. She was also trine Chiron. Venus aspecting these planets seems to recall the beginning of the myth, when Venus was no longer worshipped or venerated.

It seems that a new way of looking at the Venusian function was needed at a time when the Romantic Movement was coming to an end, and after the Uranian upheavals of the previous century. Psyche was discovered by Annibale de Gasparis, then working at the Naples Observatory. He was born in 1819, just after the Napoleonic wars, at the same time as the Italian Romantic movement (even if there were beginnings in Italy during the Napoleonic epic, Romanticism only took hold afterwards). As on the day of the discovery of the asteroid whose name he himself chose, we find in Annibale de Gasparis's chart a difficult Venus: in exile in Scorpio, she forms a 1° trine with an extremely tight triple conjunction of Saturn, Pluto and Chiron. Conjunct the Sun and Mercury, she is also trine Mars. Gasparis may therefore have had difficulty feeling his personal worth and experiencing fulfilling emotional relationships.

Neptune was discovered very shortly before Psyche, the former in September 1846 and the latter in March 1852. Both have a clear connection with the Romantic movement, which was coming to an end at the time. As Victor Hugo so aptly put it: "There has never been more talk of Romanticism than since it was said that Romanticism was dead."[8] In the previous century, the Enlightenment had laid the foundations for a paradigm shift with its emphasis on individual choice and personal happiness. In the late eighteenth and early nineteenth centuries, the Romantics were able to propose a new form of love between two people. Until then, most marriages had been governed by practical considerations (transfer of land, union between people of the same social class, agreements between families, etc.). As a result, sexuality was seen as a purely procreative or recreational activity, with no connection to love. The Romantics, on the other hand, described an ideal union, the meeting of two soul mates. Love should bring about a fusion of body and soul, of desire and feeling. It became an ideal of fulfilment, of communion between two beings.

There are many parallels between the Romantic vision of love and the one Apuleius presents through the myth of Psyche. While Cupid fell in love with Psyche's physical beauty, and Psyche physically joined him without knowing who he was, the two underwent a series of trials and transformations that allowed their union to be based on their mutual love, which was divine in nature, i.e. perfect, and on the sharing of their earthly desires, embodied in the birth of their daughter Pleasure. Psyche and Cupid are two soulmates who found the secret of happiness in the communion of hearts and bodies.

Psyche, the asteroid in the birth chart

The discovery of Psyche marks a turning point in the collective vision of what Venus represents. Until then, the astrologer who invoked Venus with their client must have been at an impasse, since Venus implies choice, and most people didn't choose their spouses. From the nineteenth century onwards, Romanticism held that happiness in marriage was possible if the partner was chosen and the two lovers wished to be united in spirit as well

---

8 Victor Hugo, *Océan – Tas de pierres* (Albin Michel, 1942).

as in body; this love bordered on the divine and brought humanity closer to a form of immortality.

In practical terms, Psyche is what makes for a truly happy union, whether in friendship or love. According to Apuleius, this asteroid guides us in developing the four pillars, which he likens to virtues, of a mature, healthy, and happy relationship. Wisdom enables us to distinguish, i.e. to respect our limits, and to discern, to make choices based on our values, without being polluted by external factors; moderation obliges us to choose the object of our affection without being subject to our senses or our bodily desires; courage enables us to take responsibility for our choices and urges us to confront our emotions and what we have ignored or repressed; finally, justice consists of not asking others to play a role we would expect of them, just as it consists of not agreeing to step outside our own destiny, and not adapting to meet the expectations of others. These are qualities that aren't readily available – otherwise, Psyche wouldn't have had to face the tasks set by Venus. We can't develop them alone by meditating or isolating ourselves: the starting point is always a relationship, because Psyche wouldn't have undertaken anything if her desire to see Cupid again hadn't been so strong. It's desire that sets us in motion, even if, as we'll see in the examples further on, it's indeed the desire to possess a part of the beauty of a loved one, because it echoes the same beauty buried deep within us. Activating Psyche and revealing the qualities she represents allows us to experience Venus genuinely, in a way that isn't obsessive, overly rational, nor tied to inherited family patterns.

The keys to interpreting Psyche in astrology

There are three keys to interpreting the asteroid Psyche in astrology: Venus, the Sun, and the notion of inner qualities whose revelation is necessary to serve them. The qualities of Psyche, symbolised by her position in signs and houses and by her aspects, are specific to each individual: it's up to us to find out how we're going to honour Venus and develop a healthy, fulfilling relationship, which "pillar" (what Apuleius called virtues) we need to work on and what our assets are to achieve this. Psyche conjunct Saturn in Virgo won't give the same information as Psyche conjunct Pluto in Cancer. While one asks us to focus on wisdom and justice, the other encourages us to have the courage to descend into Hades and confront our emotions. The sign of Psyche must find a place in our lives so our approach to relationships serves Venus and the Self. (We'll return to the interpretation of Psyche by sign in Part Three.)

If we try to schematise the inner movement, Venus pushes us into a relationship that enables us to develop the qualities symbolised by Psyche, which in turn serve the sense of self-esteem offered by Venus and her ability to bring us joy. Venus, once satisfied, gives us a sense of our own value, and can thus put herself at the service of the Sun and the meaning of our lives.

Summary

In the myth of Psyche, everything is said from the start: Venus is no longer worshipped; the goddess is no longer honoured, because her mortal copy is worshipped instead. Psyche was therefore a fake. Her labours will enable her to become real: the symbolism of the divine marriage shows that she has achieved completeness; she is now a true goddess. The soul, because it has prevented the worship of Venus, undergoes a series of works enabling it to develop attributes that it possessed but was unaware of. Similarly, through transits, progressions or cross-aspects in synastry, the activation of the asteroid Psyche enables us to develop inner qualities, which have not yet reached consciousness, necessary for the healthy and complete expression of the planet Venus.

The asteroid Psyche really deserves our attention if we understand the extent to which Venus is dependent on it. The Platonic tradition shows us that this planet, as a symbol of beauty, can be the guide to a truly initiatory path towards the divine. Astrological tradition tells us no different when it claims Venus is exalted in Pisces: in this sign, love extends to all living things, and to the divine. Thanks to her ability to bring us into relationship with a person, or with something greater than ourselves, Venus possesses both the gift of connecting us to ourselves, and to the divine.

The NASA mission

NASA launched its Psyche mission on 13 October 2023, at 10:19 a.m. EST from the Kennedy Space Center in Florida. A study of the planetary configurations at the time is particularly interesting: the Sun, Moon and Mercury are in Libra and all three are therefore ruled by Venus, which is culminating, exactly on the midheaven in Virgo. This brings us back to the emphasis on the signs of Libra and Virgo, the importance of which has already been highlighted in the myth. Regulus continues to be prominent, as it was on the day Psyche was discovered, because it's conjunct the midheaven and Venus. The sign of Scorpio is not to be outdone, as Mars is found on the first degree of the sign, reminding us that Apuleius chose to let Psyche die in the Underworld before being reborn on Olympus. In addition, Scorpio is rising, and Psyche in Sagittarius is widely conjunct the ascendant. Venus is the most important planet of the chart: conjunct the midheaven, ruler of the Sun, Moon and Mercury; she is also ruler of Uranus and Jupiter, who are in Taurus, quincunx the Sun-Mercury conjunction. Finally, Neptune is in Pisces, in the sign of exaltation of Venus, as is Saturn, on the first degree of Pisces. The presence of Saturn conjunct the chart's IC reminds us that Venus was born of the castration of Ouranos by Saturn: this divinity is at the root of Venus' very existence.

Part Two

When the Progressed Sun Shines on Psyche

Introduction

In 1852, when the asteroid was discovered, Psyche was the name of a myth dealing with self-discovery through relationship. But what about the asteroid? How can we ascertain whether it has something to do with the myth handed down by Apuleius? Howard Sasportas, the astrologer who co-founded the Centre for Psychological Astrology with Liz Greene, said he saw "the progressed Sun as a torch which shines on whatever it is touching."[9] I followed this path and discovered that meaningful events linked to relationships happen when the progressed Sun brings its light to natal Psyche. The conjunction isn't the only relevant aspect: squares, oppositions, trines, sextiles, quincunxes and even semi-sextiles are to be taken into account. It's as though the progressed Sun lit up Psyche each time it entered the degree where natal Psyche is. For example, if the asteroid is at 15° Taurus when the progressed Sun hits the same degree of every zodiac sign, an issue related to the myth of Psyche seems to emerge. The orb is quite narrow: half a degree before and after the exact aspect, which represents approximately six months before and after. The consequences can last much longer, but the relevant events and the start of the inner changes will occur within this span of one year.

The relevance of using asteroids is far from winning unanimous support. Moreover, they haven't been thoroughly studied, and there's no consensus on how to interpret them. I've gone into detail about what happened to a dozen celebrities and three of my clients when their progressed Sun lit up Psyche to convince even the most sceptical of the reality of the asteroid's effects. The events those people went through, and the changes that followed, seem to be sufficiently important to confirm the role of the asteroid.

---

9 Howard Sasportas, *Direction and Destiny in the Birth Chart* (The Wessex Astrologer, 2023).

The encounter with Psyche is a time when the way we honour Venus needs to be questioned. A relationship, whether romantic or friendly, urges us to evolve. In the myth, Venus asks her servant Care and Sorrow to torture Psyche. When the progressed Sun shines on Psyche, painful events or situations urge us to carry out our own labours to restore the cult of Venus. New inner resources come to light, and the individuation process enters an important phase. An encounter with Psyche is always a fertile moment for self-discovery.

Simone de Beauvoir

The French existentialist writer and philosopher Simone de Beauvoir provides an eloquent example of the effects of the asteroid Psyche, thanks to the diary she kept, published under the title *Diary of a Philosophy Student*.[10] This account is a unique resource for understanding the asteroid Psyche and the issues raised by a relationship of any kind when the progressed Sun forms an aspect to her. Beauvoir's Sun is at 17°31 Capricorn and her Psyche is at 10°07 Scorpio. The progressed Sun in Aquarius made an exact square to natal Psyche from 26–31 March 1930, when she was twenty-two.

Beauvoir met Jean-Paul Sartre on 8 July 1929; on 30 July they both passed their *agrégation* in philosophy, a competitive French exam required to teach at university. By September 1929, Beauvoir was already in awe of Sartre, but their relationship doesn't seem to have become intimate until October, when transiting Jupiter was on Beauvoir's natal Venus. Sartre explained, "What we have is an essential love; but it's good if we both experience contingent loves too" and offered to sign a two-year 'lease'. At the beginning of their romantic relationship, the progressed Sun was at 9°40 Aquarius, already squaring Psyche, with an orb of 0°27: it had just entered the asteroid's sphere of influence.

In the seventh notebook of her diary, the inequality of their early relationship is striking. Fascinated by Sartre, Beauvoir writes that she wants nothing more than to lose herself in him, to live only through him and for him, to forget herself so as to be happy only by the simple fact of loving him. We don't have Sartre's diary, but we can guess that he wasn't in the same frame of mind. As early as December, he warned Simone that she was far too dependent on him. Beauvoir wrote: "This is the first time, the very first time since my wonderful life started in July that I feel brutally sent away, showered with gifts, but still, dismissed forevermore." Sartre

---

10 Simone de Beauvoir, *Diary of a Philosophy Student: Volume 3, 1926-30* (University of Illinois Press, 2024).

34   In The Name of Love – The Asteroid Psyche

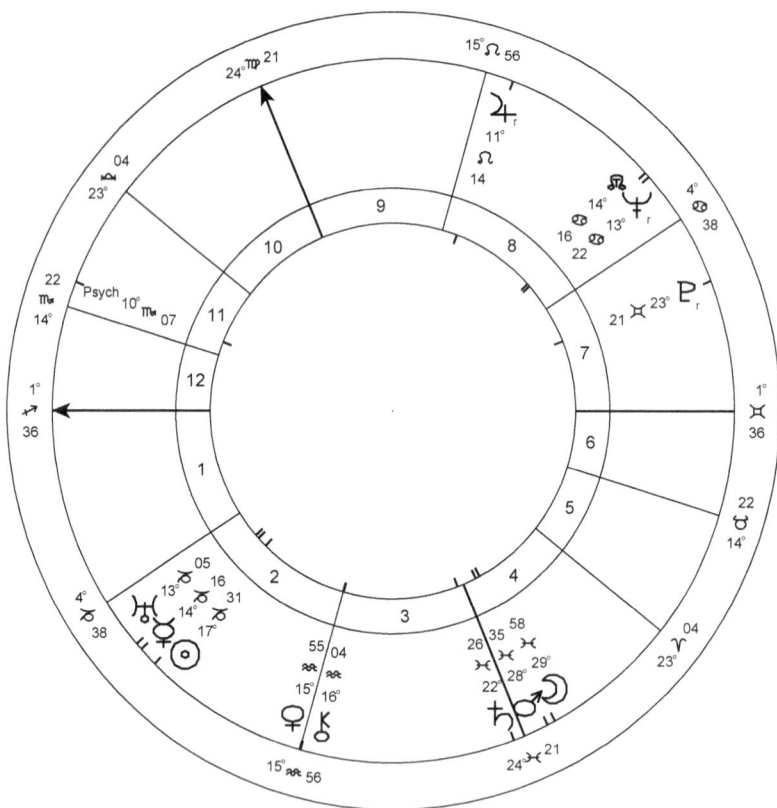

```
Name:  ♀ Simone de Beauvoir
born on Th., 9 January 1908        Time:       4:30 a.m.
in Paris, FR                       Univ.Time:  4:20:39
2e20, 48n52                        Sid. Time:  11:39:16
Natal Chart (Method: Greene Anglo / Placidus)
```

had told her that he thought she was too entrenched in her happiness. This reminds us of Psyche in her palace. The suffering of Beauvoir was great, but on the same day, she was already determined to react: "Tears from which I feel that the Valkyrie will rise, finally awakened from a long happy sleep. Yes, a little while ago I liked the feeling of being brought back in this way to the time when I had to learn everything from myself alone." On this day, 12 December, transiting Chiron was at 10°37 Taurus, squaring her natal Psyche.

Like Psyche before she decided to enlighten Cupid, the bliss in which Beauvoir lived made her forget her own goals, her own life. She lived in a kind of torpor, a happiness in which she forgot the purpose of her life, content to be loved by Sartre alone. In the same way, Psyche, who feels so alone in her palace all day and whose life consists only of waiting for her embrace with Cupid, seems to be fulfilled by this situation. Sartre sensed this, for he'd told Beauvoir the day before: "that he would like to feel that [she] could go far away from him tomorrow and not mind suffering." But they wake up: Psyche demands the truth and will find herself alone to bear the consequences through the work demanded by Venus; Beauvoir, "finally awakened from a long happy sleep", feels drawn back to herself and her potential. Yet she was unaware that her Venusian labours had only just begun.

Perhaps she had doubts about her will; on 25 December, she wondered: "Is the Valkyrie watching over me? Perhaps, from afar, and yet able to hear, but we will not call her yet, not quite yet." The year 1930 began in the same way as 1929 ended: "I don't even know what I desire. Everything is perfect. I am weak and cowardly." Psyche was still in her lover's palace, a prisoner of her bliss. The square was exact at the end of March, but Beauvoir had stopped writing and didn't resume until June. It's obvious that her Valkyrie resolutions had been in vain, since she wrote on 9 June: "As on a past December day and for almost the same reasons, I am defenceless, afraid, and overwhelmed. He reproached me in Tours yesterday for living with entirely too much dependence on him and his group. I don't know why this hurts me so." The progressed Sun was 0°12 minutes past the exact square. She knew the solution was to start writing again, but she couldn't believe in herself: "And I would love to do this, more than anything! But I don't have any talent, and I cannot! I am suffering." Venus demanded change, but Beauvoir didn't feel capable of it. Her self-esteem had suffered too much during the seven months of the relationship, and she'd lost faith in her talent.

In the myth of Psyche, it's Venus who defines the nature of labour, for it's she who is offended by the beauty of her mortal rival. In Beauvoir's chart, Venus is in Aquarius, exactly conjunct Chiron and quincunx Neptune. It's on the cusp of the third house and opposite the ruler of the ascendant, Jupiter in Leo. What such a Venus needs is not easy to summarise, but it's immediately obvious a Venus in Aquarius couldn't be satisfied with a fusional relationship in which Beauvoir would forget herself. But Neptune could. In aspect to Venus, it evokes a longing to merge with something greater than oneself. The intrapsychic conflict inherent in Beauvoir, as shown by Venus in Aquarius quincunx Neptune, was projected onto

Jean-Paul Sartre. He was both the ocean in which she wanted to drown and the one who pushed her away as soon as her Aquarian independence was threatened. Furthermore, Beauvoir's cry "But I don't have any talent" is linked to the almost exact natal conjunction between Venus, as a symbol of self-esteem, and Chiron. Since Chiron is involved, we can make an educated guess that difficulties in expressing Venus were common in her family and that there may be a self-esteem problem in the family psyche. The wound reflected by the Venus-Chiron conjunction makes Beauvoir more sensitive to the myth of Psyche in which the worship of Venus is neglected and her altars are left "bereft of offerings." Venus is on the cusp of the third house, so writing could indeed be a way of honouring the goddess. Finally, as Venus is opposite Jupiter in Leo, ruler of the ascendant, the conflict is also about how to uphold universal values (Aquarius) while allowing oneself to shine and defend a personal ambition (Leo).

In June, the relationship crisis that had started when the progressed Sun began to enlighten Psyche was still unresolved; the relationship was still unequal, Beauvoir was still forgetting herself in her love for Sartre. On 9 June, she wrote: "This love took so much, so much of everything! I so lived wanting only him as I neglected my own life!" Returning to the myth and its Platonic reading, Beauvoir had neglected the virtue of wisdom, illustrated by the work of sorting seeds, which consists in knowing how to distinguish oneself from others. Nor had she respected the virtue of temperance, as she was so excessive in her feelings. Finally, she hadn't respected justice, the Saturnian law, reflected by the exaltation of Saturn in Libra, because it requires us not to submit to others in order to play our own role and fulfil our destiny.

And yet the solution to her problems is the same, obvious but slow to take hold: "I must try to write, my only chance." Venus was in pain: "even my poor love for myself is almost dead", but now she'd realised it, she could move forward: "Don't be afraid tonight, my love; I am terribly independent from you, my love […] But if you only knew how little I care about everything, even my happiness, when I find myself again!" For Beauvoir, having the courage to find herself, and for Psyche, daring to disobey to discover the truth, involves a sacrifice: the sacrifice, at least temporarily, of the bliss experienced in love. The search for authenticity has its price.

Beauvoir stopped writing during the summer, but she resumed her diary in September, when the progressed Sun was 0°28 minutes past the exact square. She seemed to have finally found the solution to her intra-psychic conflict, projected onto her lover Jean-Paul Sartre, between love and independence, between forgetting oneself in ecstatic fusion and the search for fulfilment. She faced the truth on 6 September. Like Psyche, she shed light on her lover: "I reread my notes from last October. I sense, oh! so strongly, how much less he loved me than I loved him and how it was only a storytelling Playboy's little adventure when I, lost in awe, gave him my soul." Beauty no longer belonged to Sartre: "He is no longer as perfect in my eyes", and she'd found her inner beauty, for she wrote, on 7 September: "I could have a splendid year if I write every day like today" and, the next day: "I am happy. I wrote all day long." The cult of Venus seemed to be restored at last: writing, the expression of this Venus in Aquarius in the third house, allowed Beauvoir to rediscover her self-esteem and her joie de vivre.

Throughout the year, the qualities of her Psyche in Scorpio were revealed, allowing her to exercise the lucidity so dear to this sign of deep emotional insight to decipher what was at stake in her relationship with Sartre. Her many allusions to the Valkyrie, the warrior goddess of Germanic mythology, must be linked to the domicile of Mars in Scorpio. Moreover, as we shall see in Part Three, her Psyche is conjunct Sartre's Mars in Scorpio. It was therefore a divine beauty coloured by Mars that she'd fallen in love with, and she sensed it was by developing Martian qualities within the relationship, by drawing inspiration from a Valkyrie, that she could find herself. She finally showed herself capable of using the wisdom and courage of Scorpio to exist as a creative and authentic individual in a relationship with a man she so much admired and continued to admire throughout her life. Here we find Plato's Aphrodite-Ourania: the one who makes us fall in love with a person whose qualities mirror our own and allow us to reveal our depths. Venus in Aquarius quincunx Neptune can idealise a relationship, refusing to see that each of the protagonists has a shadow. Forced by suffering and rejection to develop the qualities symbolised by her Psyche in Scorpio, Beauvoir was able to confront her own emotional world and her dependence on Sartre in order to restore her self-esteem and values. She carried out her own labours, which consisted of revealing the qualities of Scorpio, at least, those necessary to establish a healthy and equal relationship with Sartre, like Psyche in myth. All signs have their own wisdom and can demonstrate courage and moderation in different ways; each sign can develop sufficient self-awareness to be just and to play its own role, its own destiny. Beauvoir had to do this in the way of Scorpio, and this sign evokes both the cold waters defended by the dragons of the third labour and the descent into the kingdom of Proserpine. It's easy to understand how the emotional experience she had at the age of twenty-two must have forced her to plunge into the depths of herself and left a lasting impression.

Although she couldn't know it at the time, her books gave her a symbolic immortality, and the similarity between her story and the myth of Psyche is striking. Losing oneself in love, enlightenment, suffering, labours, the search for wholeness, immortality: all the elements of the myth are there. Beauvoir's romantic life is a wonderful expression of what is required of us when we deal with Psyche: "I am myself, with my life, my desires, my friends, my work to do, and I love him." When the progressed Sun hits Psyche, a break-up is possible and, as we shall see, happens quite often. But it's not obligatory: Beauvoir and Sartre didn't break up. Beauvoir brilliantly shows us how to use the lessons of the asteroid and honour Venus without abandoning the relationship through which they were passed on. When Beauvoir wrote: "I am no longer that little girl full of adventures and dreams", something died in her, like Psyche after opening Persephone's box; but the autonomous and independent writer attained immortality.

Friedrich Nietzsche

The philosopher Friedrich Nietzsche underwent a decisive rupture when his progressed Sun was sextile his natal Psyche in July 1878. It could be argued that this was a turning point in his life, work and thought. At that time, Nietzsche believed he'd found the answers to the metaphysical questions that haunted him in the music of Richard Wagner. He wrote, in 1876, in *Untimely Meditations,* that Wagner "can be called a simplifier of the world, for simplification of the world consists in being able to view and thus master the tremendous abundance of an apparently chaotic wilderness" in an attempt to explain his art and make people understand its unique scope.[11]

After reading Nietzsche's work, Wagner was delighted and wrote to Nietzsche that he'd understood him extraordinarily well. Cosima Wagner, his wife, insisted that Nietzsche should come to see the rehearsals and then assist at the premieres of his Bayreuth Festival, which was to take place in the summer of 1876. Nietzsche agreed, despite his health problems, but soon wished he hadn't: Wagner had no time for him, he suffered from terrible headaches, and he began to doubt. Not about Wagner's music itself, but the people who loved it. His criticism was of the Wagnerians, not of Wagner. In the autumn of 1876, Nietzsche and the Wagners spent their holidays in the same Italian town and saw each other every day, either at Nietzsche's or Wagner's house. They took long walks, during which they talked a great deal about philosophy and their respective points of view. Nietzsche, who had lost his father when he was a young child, needed a substitute. He'd found in Wagner someone older whom he could admire, who cared for him and his health, and whose wife treated him like family. His relationship with Wagner was therefore the most important relationship of his life, and remained so after their separation, even after his death, for Nietzsche wrote in *Nietzsche contra Wagner*: "For I had no one save

---

11 Friedrich Nietzsche, *Untimely Meditations* (Cambridge University Press, 1997).

In The Name of Love – The Asteroid Psyche

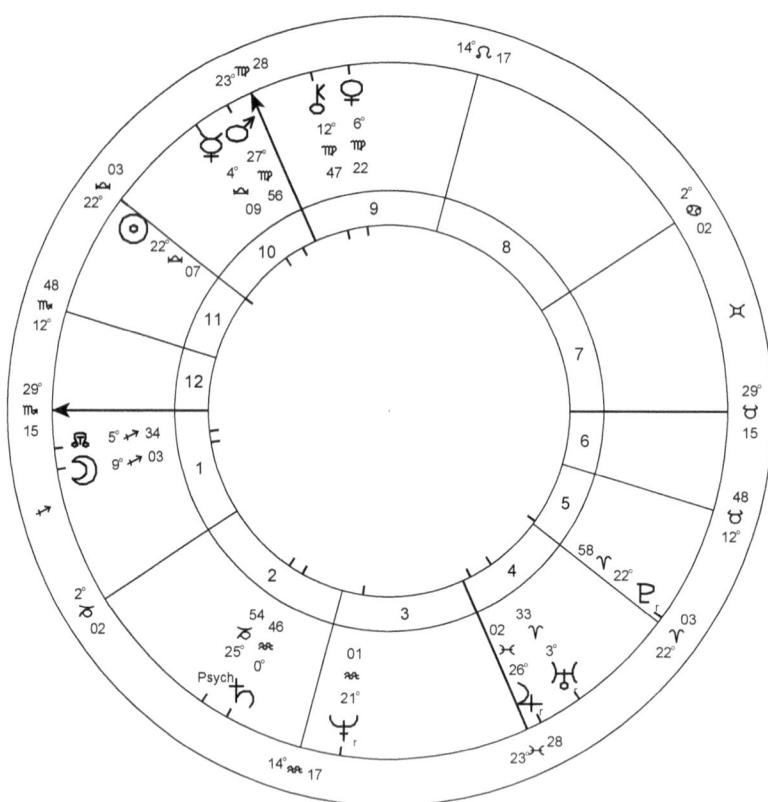

Richard Wagner" and, in *the Case of Wagner*: "To turn my back on Wagner was for me a fate; to like anything at all again after that, a triumph."

In 1877, as he later explained, Nietzsche had many doubts about Wagner's art, but he remained faithful. In October he wrote to Cosima that it was a great comfort for him to know that his next opera, *Parsifal*, would soon be finished. But two months later, in January 1878, and as his progressed Sun began to sextile Psyche, with an orb of 0°30, he finished *Human, all too Human*. In this book, although Wagner wasn't explicitly mentioned, he recognised that he'd changed his mind about music: it was no longer a meaningful language and should be given a secondary place in the hierarchy of the arts. Moreover, some of his aphorisms alluded to Cosima Wagner and were unflattering to her and her husband. When he sent his book to Wagner in April, he knew he would lose his friendship. According to Cosima Wagner's diary, Wagner didn't open it at that time, but waited until 24 June.[12] On that very day, Nietzsche's progressed Sun was almost exactly sextile Psyche, with an orb of 0°02. Cosima wrote that her husband was "surprised by his conceited vulgarity." Their relationship was over; they never spoke again.

On 15 July, Nietzsche wrote to his friend Mathilda Maier, explaining that this year had been a turning point in his life: "I now live my aspiration to wisdom, down to the smallest detail, whereas earlier I only revered and idolized the wise—briefly, if you could only know how it feels to have known this change and this crisis, then you could not avoid wishing to have such an experience yourself." The parallels with the myth of Psyche are striking: Psyche desperately searched for the divine beauty she saw in Cupid, and ultimately embodied that beauty by being granted immortality. Nietzsche thought he'd found the wise and eventually discovered that wisdom was his inner beauty. Shortly before sinking into madness, the philosopher returned to this period of his life in *Nietzsche contra Wagner*: "As I continued my journey alone, I trembled. Not long after this I was ill, more than ill—I was tired [...] by the sadness of a ruthless suspicion—that I was now condemned to be ever more and more suspicious, ever more and more contemptuous, ever more and more deeply alone than I had been theretofore." For him, the Venusian labours were particularly cruel, for he had to resign himself to loneliness and solitude, and to the mistrust he already knew and feared, having been confronted with it during his teenage years and his studies.

Throughout this period, transiting Pluto opposed Nietzsche's progressed Sun: from May to September 1878, the aspect was very close. The *kairos* (the colour of time) was Plutonian: a period of renunciation of structures, ideals, thoughts, and relationships that no longer served a person's evolution but, on the contrary, kept them stuck in an old skin that had become too tight. This transit is reminiscent of the shedding of the skin of the snake, a cold-blooded animal whose symbolic links with the unconscious are evocative of those of the planet Pluto. This transit was of course of great importance in Nietzsche's life, in 1878. But the asteroid

---

12 Cosima Wagner, *Cosima Wagner's Diaries, Vol. 2: 1878-1883* (A Helen and Kurt Wolff Book/Harcourt Brace Jovanovich, 1978).

Psyche, like Mars, often acts as a trigger, a revealer, for the transits of the outer planets, as we shall see in Part Three. In the case of the philosopher, it's clear that his separation from Wagner, orchestrated by Venus and leading to the revelation of his Psychean qualities, was a moment of outward manifestation of the profound mutation symbolised by the transit of Pluto. And this separation occurred at the exact moment of the sextile between the progressed Sun and Psyche.

In Nietzsche's birth chart, the Sun is in Libra squaring Psyche, trine Neptune (1°06), and the nodal axis is on the ascendant-descendant axis. This suggests, to say the least, that relationships were of paramount importance in the construction of his identity. The trine to Neptune evokes his tendency toward idealisation and then disillusionment. As noted above, when the progressed Sun makes an aspect to Psyche, it's time to question the way in which we have honoured Venus in our lives to date. In Nietzsche's chart, Venus is the ruler of the Sun in Libra. The planet is in Virgo and in the ninth house. Virgo is an invitation to choice, discernment, and inner integrity, whereas Nietzsche "idolized the wise" rather than seeking his own wisdom. He followed a surrogate father rather than stand by his own thinking. The ninth house is where Venus's 'altars' are: philosophy, thoughts, ideas and social groups. Venus conjoins Chiron: Nietzsche's self-esteem may have been low, at least early in his life. According to the myth of Chiron and the symbol of the wounded healer, relationships can cause both eternal wounds and healing. This conjunction may also suggest that solitude, which wounds the Venusian need for relationships, may be necessary to build a strong sense of self-worth. Psyche is in Capricorn conjunct Saturn: the qualities that may have emerged in 1878 are those of the ability to accept temporary isolation, to be self-reliant, to embody the guide, the expert, the wise man and the Father principle. Capricorn allowed Nietzsche to think without external support and to access the virtues of Platonic wisdom and justice, which consist in being true to oneself without depending on others or expecting their approval. His Psychean qualities gave him access to his uprightness.

Nietzsche needed to find his inner beauty, the qualities of his Psyche, to build solid boundaries (Virgo) between his thoughts (ninth house) and those of others, including Wagner. His thinking had to be as pure as possible, cleansed of any influence and any admiration, getting rid of any loyalty or fidelity to a father substitute. Psyche in Capricorn allowed him to honour Venus. His break with Wagner may seem like a renunciation, but it was essential for Nietzsche and his Venus in Virgo. Never again would he allow himself to idealise anyone, or to seek answers to his own questions in the thoughts of others. And he always referred to this period of his life as a crisis, a time of great suffering that allowed his soul and his thought to heal.

John Lennon

There are similarities between the musician John Lennon and Nietzsche, two men who lived almost a hundred years apart. In Lennon's birth chart, Venus is in Virgo, the Sun is in Libra, and there is an exact trine between Psyche and the Sun. The importance of relationships is underlined again, and the myth of Psyche is emphasised by the trine between the asteroid and the Sun, and because Venus rules Libra. The encounter between Lennon's progressed Sun and Psyche led to a process strikingly similar to that which produced the split between Nietzsche and Wagner. Again, the divergence had begun earlier, but reached the point of no return at the moment of contact with the asteroid. And in this case too, the relationship was of major importance: that with Paul McCartney.

Lennon's progressed Sun, then in Scorpio, made an exact quincunx to Psyche from 13–19 November 1970. This was a very peculiar year for him: the year of The Beatles' break-up and the year of his less known therapy with Arthur Janov: a primal therapy, named after Janov's book *The Primal Scream*. Lennon went to Los Angeles with his wife Yoko Ono to undergo this therapy for three months, from May to July 1970. As soon as he returned to England, he recorded what would become a legendary album: *John Lennon and Plastic Ono Band*. During the recording, from 26 September to 23 October, the quincunx between the progressed Sun and Psyche was very close, with an orb of 0°08. The album deals with Lennon's traumas: the fact that his mother abandoned him (they managed to build a relationship during Lennon's teenage years, but she died when he was seventeen), the problems with his father, the working class background of his family, and the end of The Beatles.

For a man whose natal trine between the Sun and Psyche echoes the quincunx between the progressed Sun and the asteroid, this moment in his life seems to have been the kairos, the opportune time to face the suffering associated with the first relationships of his life: "Janov showed me how to feel my own fear and pain, therefore I can handle it better than I could before, that's all [...] Because before, I wasn't feeling things, that's all. I was blocking the feelings, and when the feelings come through, you cry", he confessed in *Rolling Stone* in December 1970.[13] Transiting Jupiter was trine his progressed Moon and square his natal Moon in Aquarius in September. There's no doubt this helped him to renew the way he lived and expressed his feelings. But language played an extremely important role in Lennon's development at that point. His Psyche is in Gemini and in the second house, which, as well as symbolising our values or our relationship with the body, is linked to primary narcissism. According to Freud, through the reception a child receives from his parents and their "compulsion to attribute to the child all the perfections", he became the repository of their long-abandoned narcissism.[14] Lennon, whose relationship with his parents was complicated from the start, had to question this primary narcissism at a time when his progressed Sun was shining on Psyche. His primal therapy and the writing of new songs enabled him to let his feelings out, which was essential in order to be able to honour Venus. It was here that Lennon truly completed the third work of Psyche, daring to plunge into the dark and icy waters of emotion and developing the courage that Gemini gives to confront the unconscious with words.

The main transits at that time were related to Venus: transiting Uranus conjunct progressed Venus and transiting Chiron square progressed Venus. Uranus had already made a first conjunction to progressed Venus in early 1970, and Chiron a first square to Psyche in April, but the time when a significant relationship would break out was set by Psyche: on 15 November, the day Paul McCartney filed a lawsuit against him. Psyche accelerates ongoing changes during transits of slow-moving planets: like Mars, she acts as a trigger, a spark. So, the worst was yet to come, for Venus expected Lennon to do some very painful work. He had to come clean about his relationship with McCartney. Apart from Yoko Ono, no one had played such an important role in John Lennon's life as McCartney. Right up until his death, Lennon talked about him in almost every interview he gave. Looking at their charts, the almost exact square between Lennon's

---

13 Jann S. Wenner. *Lennon remembers: The Full Rolling Stone Interviews from 1970* (New York: Verso, 2000).
14 Sigmund Freud, *On Narcissism : An introduction*, in *The Standard Edition of the Complete Psychological Works of Sigmund Freud*, Vol.14 (1914-1916) (Hogarth Press 1957).

46 In The Name of Love – The Asteroid Psyche

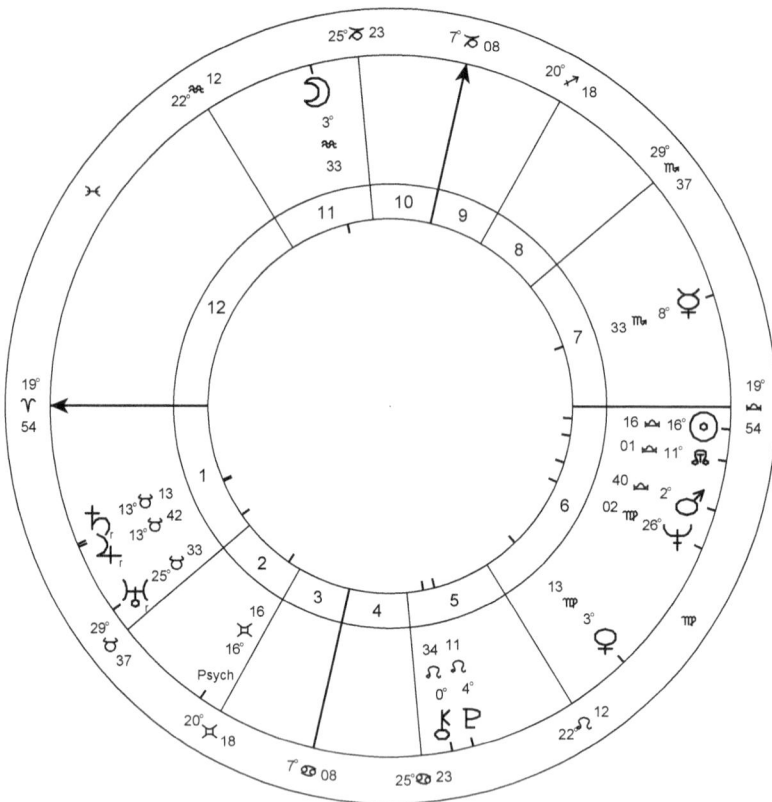

Name: ♂ John Lennon
born on We., 9 October 1940
in Liverpool, ENG (UK)
2w55, 53n25
Time: 6:30 p.m.
Univ.Time: 17:30
Sid. Time: 18:31:03
Natal Chart (Method: Greene Anglo / Placidus)

Neptune and McCartney's Sun in Gemini is striking. Lennon probably admired his friend's talent and sharp wit, as well as his eclecticism. But there was also a risk of disappointment.

In September 1969, after a successful concert with Ono, Lennon decided to leave The Beatles. But it was kept secret for financial reasons, and McCartney finally revealed it in April 1970. For him, there was a huge problem: the liquidation of The Beatles. Under pressure from Lennon, they'd chosen Allen Klein as their new manager, with whom McCartney had refused to sign a contract. He didn't think Klein was honest and would have preferred his own brother-in-law John Eastman. Ringo Starr and George Harrison decided to listen to Lennon, and Klein was appointed manager by three of the four Beatles. Now he knew The Beatles were over,

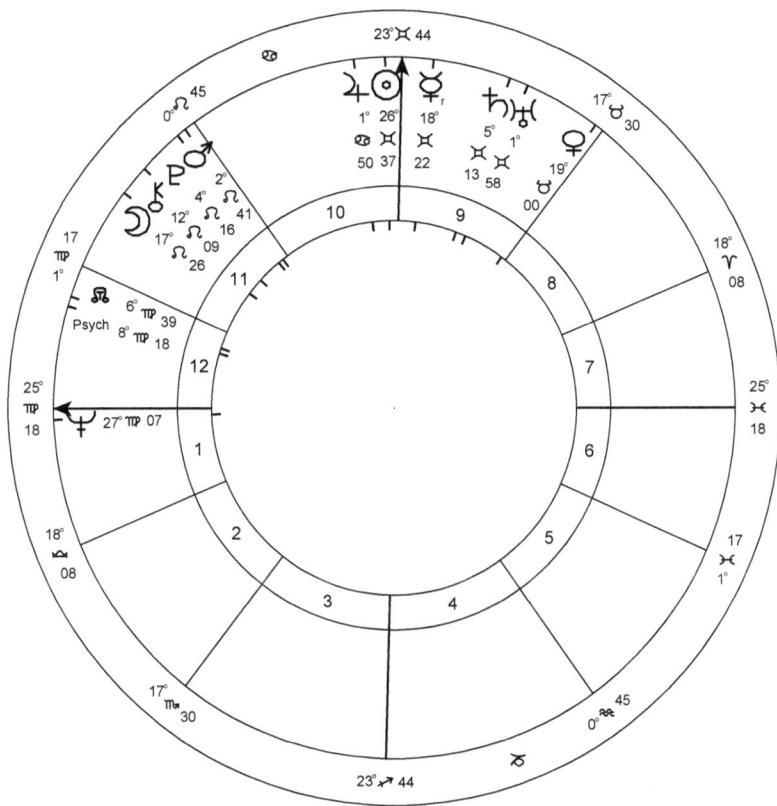

McCartney wanted their partnership dissolved as soon as possible, because he thought the way Klein was handling their money was dangerous and that the man was toxic. He tried to get the agreement of the other three, but when he didn't get any support, he filed a lawsuit against them through his lawyers. The damage was done, and it was irreversible. That very day, 15 November, Lennon's progressed Sun made an exact quincunx to his natal Psyche. McCartney attempted a final reconciliation with Harrison, but having failed, he sued the three other Beatles in the High Court in London in December.

For Lennon, experiencing the asteroid Psyche meant being sued by his best friend, his lifelong partner, the one with whom he'd experienced unparalleled success. Suddenly, the light that illuminated McCartney made him look different, and probably terribly disappointing. Lennon gave an interview to *Rolling Stone* in December 1970, in which we can understand how he reacted to this earthquake. First he complained about McCartney's leadership of the band. Their separation had freed him to record the best songs of his life: "I think it's the best thing I've ever done. I think it's realistic and it's true to me."[15] This very long interview with Jan Wenner, published in two separate issues of *Rolling Stone*, shows the new importance Lennon attached to language, to communicating who he was, and the revelation of the virtues of his Psyche in Gemini.

In Lennon's chart, Venus is in the sign of her fall, Virgo, in the sixth house. Venusian issues are therefore at stake at work and in work relationships. Venus is square Uranus: it seems that Lennon was honouring such a Venus when he said in the same interview that he didn't want to be part of a group anymore, preferring to play with different people at different times. Venus in Virgo emphasises the need to distinguish between what is ours and what is someone else's: there's a longing for purity in personal choices and values. In Lennon's chart, Neptune, with his innate desire to merge, is conjunct Mars, the ruler of the ascendant. The discriminating qualities of Venus in Virgo are therefore much needed to avoid confusion between one's own desires and those of others. By recording an album without The Beatles, Lennon was able to be true to himself, to become an individual, to make his music sound the way he wanted it to sound and to express what he wanted to express.

Words are the tool John used to help Venus in Virgo restore her purity and boundaries. He set things right: "But now I'm sick of reading things that say Paul is the musician and George is the philosopher. I wonder where I fit in, what was my contribution? I get hurt, you know [...] I'm standing by my work whereas before I would not stand by it." And when asked whether he was a genius: "Yes, if there is such a thing as one, I am one." Lennon stood by his work and was true to himself; he was successful in achieving the labours set by Venus, and had unveiled his Psychean qualities. Note the use of the word "faithful" twice: there's a clear connection here with Virgo discernment and the first work of Psyche, but also with justice and

---

15 Jann S. Wenner. *Lennon remembers: The Full Rolling Stone Interviews from 1970* (New York: Verso, 2000).

the final labour. Lennon revealed himself by separating from McCartney, using the talents of his Psyche in Gemini, his mastery and love of language, to complete his metamorphosis. When he was stuck with McCartney and The Beatles, he couldn't follow his own path, and he was probably very impressed by McCartney's talent and The Beatles' fame. Psyche helped him to break the bonds that kept him static and discover his inner beauty, his immortality. Every encounter with Psyche is a chance to become truer to oneself, to become more complete, to glimpse something in oneself we have pursued in someone else. McCartney's talent and beauty, as shown by his stellium in Gemini, echoed Lennon's Psyche in the same sign, as we shall see in Part Three.

On 12 March 1971, McCartney won the lawsuit. Lennon's progressed Sun was still within orb of Psyche during the first half of the year, and he experienced much distress over the dissolution of The Beatles' partnership. But when the progressed Sun left Psyche in June, he began recording the album *Imagine*. He settled some scores with McCartney on "How Do You Sleep?" But above all, he wrote his most famous song "Imagine", a pacifist and universalist anthem. In France, the day after the attacks of 11 September, every radio played this song at the same time, and Neil Young performed it during the benefit concert *America: A Tribute to Heroes*. This album also includes "Gimme Some Truth" and "I Don't Want To Be a Soldier", which are scathing criticisms of politicians and war. While the 1970 album, recorded after his primal therapy, dealt mainly with Lennon's traumas, the 1971 album *Imagine* allowed him to dwell on social themes, commitments, and fights. These were topics McCartney didn't want to deal with. The separation from his best friend was an unforgettable trauma, but it allowed Lennon to express himself in a way he couldn't have dreamed of if he'd stayed in The Beatles and tried to please McCartney as he had before.

Camille

One of my clients, Camille, also began therapy when her progressed Sun was coming up to conjoin Psyche. Her progressed Sun was in Cancer, a sign that favours inwardness, self-care and inner-child listening. She was able to express her suffering in relation to her relationship with her mother, who was chronically depressed and didn't pay attention to her. She hadn't been able to face this trauma before and was constantly questioning her relationship with her father, who wasn't perfect but at least tried to build a relationship with his daughter. As a teenager, she directed her anger at him, not her mother, because she knew he could handle it. But in 2017 it was the kairos, the right time to deal with what she'd been denied as a child, as indicated in the birth chart by a cardinal grand cross involving the Moon in Capricorn, a Mars-Saturn conjunction in late Cancer and early Leo, Chiron in Aries and Uranus in Libra.

It would be an understatement to say that her Venus in Taurus wasn't honoured in her marriage: instead of savouring the simple joys of life, the sensuality and pleasure of sharing daily life with her loved one, Camille was constantly on her guard, afraid of upsetting her husband. Taurus seeks relaxation in a relationship, the kind that comes from feeling at ease in the here and now with the other person, while Camille was always under tension. Venus's taste for beauty wasn't respected either, because, used to ignoring her needs and instincts, Camille had never sought to know what she really found beautiful and what she genuinely liked.

The inner work allowed her to enlighten her relationship with her husband, which was very much like the one she had with her mother. The exact conjunction of the progressed Sun and Psyche occurred when she began to realise she should get a divorce. Two months later, a series of violent confrontations with her husband hastened her decision: holidays during which he was constantly tense and verbally violent, a palpable tension throughout the day, and finally, in a move that seemed irreversible, he threw one of her twins on her bed, frightening them both. When she heard her little girls crying, she knew it was over. The lamp had shed light on her husband and she no longer thought he was the beautiful one, the one with talent and intelligence, the one she should listen to. She began to seek help. It wasn't easy, but she found her way out and began to honour Venus. This separation allowed her to reconnect with herself and finally begin to listen to her desires.

Camille's Psyche, in Cancer, is exactly square her ex-husband's Chiron, in Aries. Her ascendant is also in Cancer, as is Saturn, as mentioned earlier. Saturn in Cancer and the Moon, ruler of this sign, at the heart of the cardinal cross, suggest that Camille, in order to be true to her Cancer ascendant, had to revisit her early childhood and the wounds of which she was unaware. Psyche in Cancer indicates she needed to develop the qualities of this sign, particularly its wisdom, in order to fully live her Venus in Taurus in the eleventh house. Cancer prefers to move sideways and its wisdom lies in its ability to retrace its steps, to walk in the footsteps of its past. The Moon, whose memory is said to be very long, rules this sign. A coin minted during the reign of the Emperor Augustus shows a crab, symbol of Cancer, holding a butterfly in its claws, symbol of the soul and thus of the asteroid Psyche. The link between Cancer and Psyche is therefore a special one; some Pythagoreans took up an older theory (the origin of which is unknown) according to which the soul descends from the Milky Way to incarnate on Earth through the door of Cancer and then, at the end of its earthly life, returns to Heaven through the door of Capricorn. Cancer would therefore be the sign that welcomes and cares for the soul at the beginning. Psyche in Cancer is therefore an invitation to return to our origins, to the beginnings of life, to understand what was lacking in early childhood, and to succeed in giving the soul the welcome it needed.

We can understand why she thought she had found a way to heal and develop the qualities of Cancer by choosing a husband with Chiron exactly square her Psyche: her husband's wound triggered her own inner self. Interactions in synastry involving Chiron are never simple and can't be described a priori: everything depends on the degree of awareness of the two people. In this case, it seems that the arrival of the progressed Sun on Psyche, in square to her husband's Chiron, enabled Camille to feel the wound of her inner child sufficiently to commit herself to therapy. She was then able to deal with her husband's increasingly aggressive behaviour. It was time for her to use the wisdom of Cancer to protect herself and create the conditions she needed to flourish. There followed a period of peacefulness, favourable to the satisfaction of her Venus in Taurus, during which she devoted herself to embellishing her home and redefining her values. As with Lennon, the enlightenment of Psyche by the progressed Sun manifested itself in her entry into therapy, followed by the end of an extremely important relationship. But the Lennon-McCartney break-up had nothing to do with Lennon's therapy, since it was McCartney who initiated it. Similarly, Camille's husband was much more violent than usual, even though she was finally ready to face him. So it's a question of synchronicity, not causality, and it would seem that the disturbing behaviour of a loved one, like a re-examination of early childhood trauma, are two different ways in which the asteroid can make us question the way on which we've experienced Venus.

Two years later, Camille was able to start a new relationship with a man she'd truly chosen because of his qualities and because he corresponded with her values. She was able to use the lessons she'd learned from Psyche to build a relationship that would be a source of harmony and joy in her life, but also one that would support her self-confidence, enabling her to invest in new projects, to dare to express who she was and to live her Sun more fully.

Madame du Châtelet

Emilie du Châtelet was a French scientist, the first to make a name for herself in the field of physics and metaphysics. When her progressed Sun hit her natal Psyche, it wasn't an emotional relationship that was at stake, but a master-disciple bond. It was no less painful for a woman who placed knowledge above all other values, including love.

Born in Paris in the early eighteenth century, Gabrielle Émilie du Chastelet, known as Émilie du Châtelet, was fortunate to have a father who made little distinction between the education of his sons and of his daughter. From a very early age she showed "a dominant taste for mathematics and metaphysics" and her father, the Baron de Breteuil, had her educated at home in these two subjects instead of sending her to a convent.[16] She received a thorough education in languages, which gave her a perfect command of Latin, as well as in science and philosophy. She became a great intellectual, a Cartesian whose only way of thinking was deduction. For Voltaire, the French writer and philosopher of the Enlightenment, who was her lover and intellectual companion, she was remarkable for "the severe firmness and vigorous temper of her mind."

Châtelet slept little, worked a lot and displayed extraordinary intellectual abilities. However, despite her ambition and solid education, she couldn't reach the level of the male students who graduated from university and then worked under the guidance of a master. In fact, she was limited by her solitary work. She therefore called upon the best scientists of her time, namely Maupertuis, Clairaut and Johann Samuel Koenig, a German mathematician. By the time her progressed Sun illuminated Psyche, she'd begun to study with the latter.

The time of Châtelet's birth isn't known, and the date of the exact quincunx between her progressed Sun and Psyche can't be determined

---

16 Voltaire, "Mémoires pour servir à la vie de Monsieur de Voltaire" in *Œuvres complètes de Voltaire*, ed. Beuchot, Vol. I (Garnier Frères, 1883, p.7).

with precision: we can be sure, however, that it was in 1739, whatever the time of birth. If we take a midday birth, we get an exact quincunx in the middle of May 1739. We know what this period in Châtelet's life was like thanks to her correspondence, particularly with her former teacher and ex-lover Maupertuis, with whom she'd remained friends.[17] On 11 May, 1739, Châtelet went to Brussels with Voltaire to settle an inheritance dispute concerning her husband, and she was delighted: "I came here the strongest by bringing M. de Voltaire and M. de Koenig." Koenig had arrived at her home on 27 April.

But on 20 June, she told Maupertuis of her difficulties and deep doubts about her value as a woman of science, saying: "I don't really know if Koenig wants to do anything with me, I think my incapacity disgusts him." She continued: "I'm afraid it's very late for me to learn so many difficult things." Yet Mme du Châtelet needed these lessons. Four months earlier, she'd written: "I am going to leave physics for a while for geometry, the key to all doors." This was clearly a very painful moment in Émilie's life: her teachers had always praised her scientific intelligence, considering it superior to Voltaire's, and she'd always managed to reach the level she wanted in her studies. To keep up with Koenig, she spared no effort, getting up every day at six in the morning, despite her late bedtime, but she became discouraged: "Sometimes I'm ready to give up everything."

In Émilie du Châtelet's chart, Venus in Aquarius makes no major aspect other than an opposition to Uranus. Her self-esteem was based on her independence of thought and the acquisition of what she valued: abstract and universal knowledge. In her life, Aquarius never manifested itself in a need for brotherhood or a desire to improve the lot of her fellow human beings. Rather, she demonstrated the selfishness necessary for the success of the work she left us, in particular her annotated translations of Newton's *Principia* and her explanation of Leibniz's doctrine. In her relationship with Koenig, Châtelet showed neither the independence of mind nor the necessary distance so dear to her Venus in Aquarius opposite Uranus. In general terms, she'd hitherto been content in her work to act as Voltaire's interlocutor: he relied on her to discuss and enrich his own work – sometimes they worked separately and then compared their results by the fireside. But Émilie didn't publish under her own name and hadn't yet

---

17 Émilie du Châtelet, *La Correspondance d'Émilie Du Châtelet 1733-1740* (Centre international d'étude du XVIIIe siècle 2018).

Name: ♀ Emilie du Châtelet
born on Fr., 17 December 1706
in Paris, FR
2e20, 48n52

Time: 12:00 p.m. LMT hyp.
Univ.Time: 11:50:40

Natal Chart (Method: Greene Anglo / Placidus)

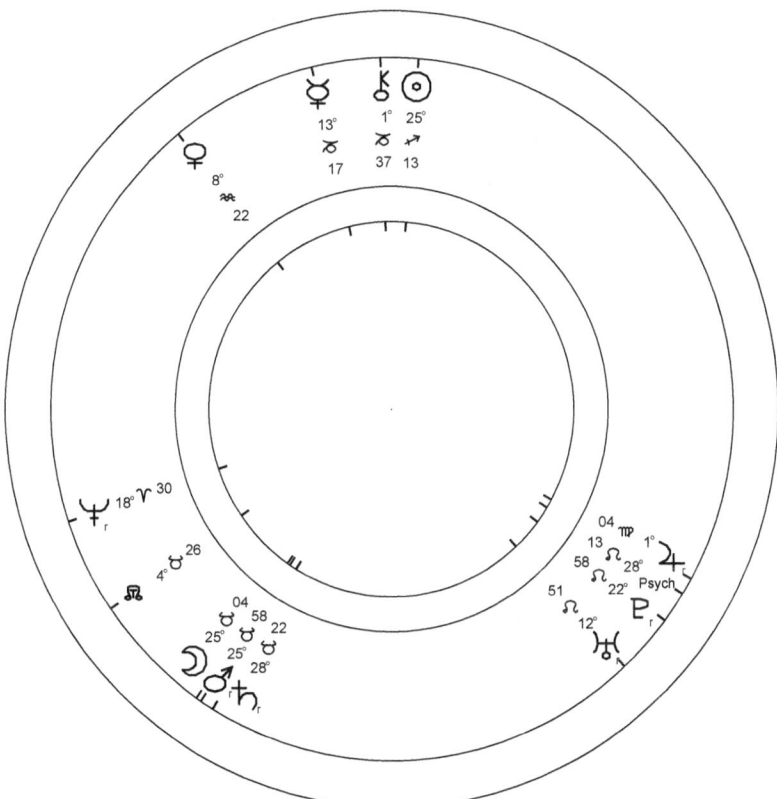

dared to express personal opinions on subjects that Voltaire hadn't chosen to study. The encounter with the asteroid Psyche was therefore an opportunity to pay a more authentic homage to her Venus. But first she had to suffer and doubt her own worth.

In June 1739, faced with what looked like failure, her self-confidence was at its lowest ebb: "I confess to you that one of the most sensitive sorrows I have had in my life is the despair I am ready to enter into over my capacity for a science which is the only one I love." In September, however, she began to pull herself together, and to understand that the failure was Koenig's fault, and not hers: "I cannot guess what his plan was in coming to me, for even if I had been an angel it would have been impossible for me in three months of travel and business to learn what I wanted to know."

Anger was rising, not at herself but at him: "I must tell you that M. de Koenig's behaviour would make me hate all mathematicians."

At the end of 1739, Châtelet tried unsuccessfully to persuade Johann Bernoulli, a Swiss mathematician and physicist, to replace Koenig in Brussels. Her letters to Bernoulli show that something serious had happened between her and Koenig that autumn: "He took so much trouble to prove to me that he had the soul of an ill-bred lackey that I had to see him for what he is [...] It is impossible for you to imagine, Sir, the indignity and lowliness of his treatment of me." Unfortunately for Émilie, Koenig had so sullied her reputation that even Maupertuis, a faithful friend, discouraged Bernoulli from giving her lessons, and Châtelet had to continue her education and study of Leibniz on her own. We can't fail to notice in the quoted extract the phrase "I had to see him for what he is", which recalls the unveiling at the heart of the myth of Psyche. Châtelet had put Koenig on a pedestal and asked him to feed her with knowledge, without asking herself whether he was capable of doing so or whether he was worth the trouble. Like Psyche in Cupid's palace, she waited impatiently for her master, admiring him without really knowing him.

Her collaboration with Koenig remained a very bad memory for her and caused her grief until 1741, when he accused her of plagiarism. But this wasn't a lost moment in her life. On the contrary, a year earlier she'd begun writing a book that was published three years later under the title *Foundations of Physics*. Thanks to Koenig, who had introduced her to Leibniz, in 1739 she returned to the book, then in print, to add what made it so valuable: her explanations of Leibniz's theories. Although Koenig accused her of taking over a book he'd written for her, Châtelet was proved right, and this work is now often regarded as her greatest. It's said that Einstein referred to it when he wrote his famous $E=mc^2$, for she was the only one who understood where Newton was wrong and Leibniz was right.

Her failure with Koenig taught her a great deal about herself: she understood that she could be successful on her own, and she could take positions that might bring her rejection from her community. In her chart, Psyche is in Leo. She therefore had to develop the qualities of Leo in order to honour Venus and, by extension, her Sun. She took the risk of expressing a personal point of view, of speaking in her own name and no longer hiding behind the talent of others. With her Sun in Sagittarius and her Venus in Aquarius, the meaning she gave to her life, her raison d'être, what made her feel worthwhile, came from understanding the laws of the universe. With her eyes riveted to the heavens, she had to remember to shine her own light. She had to take the risk of speaking in the first person, while at the same time presenting collective and universal knowledge and expressing what made her different and original as a scientist. Thanks to the courage and wisdom of Leo, she re-established the cult of Venus in Aquarius opposite Uranus. She felt legitimate in the theoretical scientific knowledge that is so dear to Aquarius, and no longer allowed any scientist to make her doubt her worth. It's interesting that the asteroid was exactly square Saturn on the day of her birth: this shows the importance of a Master in helping her to unfold the qualities symbolised by Psyche. Koenig played a major role here, but Maupertuis had played a similar one before him. After this encounter with Psyche, Châtelet took on a new dimension by publishing her *Foundations of Physics*, allowing herself to defend her personal ambitions and opinions. The controversy that followed the publication of this work on the "living forces" brought her into conflict with the secretary of the Academy of Sciences, and she was supported only by Maupertuis, while even Voltaire distanced himself. But Châtelet was able to respond to the most ardent critics, to justify a personal point of view, and to win: "I am not a secretary, but I am right, and that is worth all the titles", she wrote to a friend in 1741.[18] There is no doubt that her Venus must have felt honoured, and that her relationship with Koenig marked a decisive turning point in her personal development.

Finally, in a book that aims at highlighting the interest of studying asteroids, it may be worth mentioning that Asteroid 12059 was named *du Châtelet* in her honour. When we think of the person to whom Émilie was most important and on whom she had the greatest influence, one name stands out: Voltaire, for whom she was lover, collaborator, inspirer, corrector, guide and very dear friend. In his chart, Voltaire has a conjunction with an orb of less than 1 degree between his Sun and the du Châtelet asteroid. Voltaire also has an asteroid of his own, 5676. In Châtelet's chart, Asteroid 5676 is at 25°45 Libra, in an almost exact sextile to her Sun at 25°13 Sagittarius. It was Voltaire who fought to preserve her legacy by publishing her work on Newton after her death.

---

18 Letter to the Comte d'Argental, 2 May 1741.

Isaac Newton

A few words on Isaac Newton, whose *Principia* were so perfectly explained by Émilie du Châtelet, although it may seem complicated to study the effect of the progressed Sun in aspect to Psyche in the life of this great physicist, who never married, had no known affair, and is thought to have had a form of high functioning autism, which isolated him socially.

We do know of at least one friend of Newton's (or at least one significant relationship): the colleague with whom he lived at Trinity College, John Wickins. This cohabitation was a milestone in Newton's life for twenty years. Wickins left Trinity College in 1684, and the date of his new appointment, 4 April 1684, is known. The Cambridge University website gives the same date for Wickins' departure. The exact trine between the progressed Sun and Psyche occurred in September 1684. It's therefore quite possible that the loss of his only friend was the event that forced the physicist to reveal the qualities of his Psyche in Libra. We have no written record of Newton's relationship with Wickins, but the loss of this friendship is similar to the earthquakes experienced by Nietzsche and Lennon.

Shortly before the exact trine, in August 1684, Edmond Halley, the astronomer who discovered the comet of the same name, paid him a visit. He came to ask him what the curve of the orbit of a celestial body around the Sun would be if the gravitational pull of the star were proportional to the square of the distance from the body. "An ellipse",[19] replied Newton. He knew this because he'd calculated it, but it was impossible for him to get his hands on his calculations to give to Halley, so he promised to send them to him. Once he found them, he wanted to do the calculations again, because he wasn't satisfied with them. What he felt at the time, when his progressed Sun was trine Psyche, must have been similar to what Madame

---

19 Derek T. Whiteside, *The Preliminary Manuscript for Isaac Newton's 1687 Principia, 1684-1685* (Cambridge University Press, 1989).

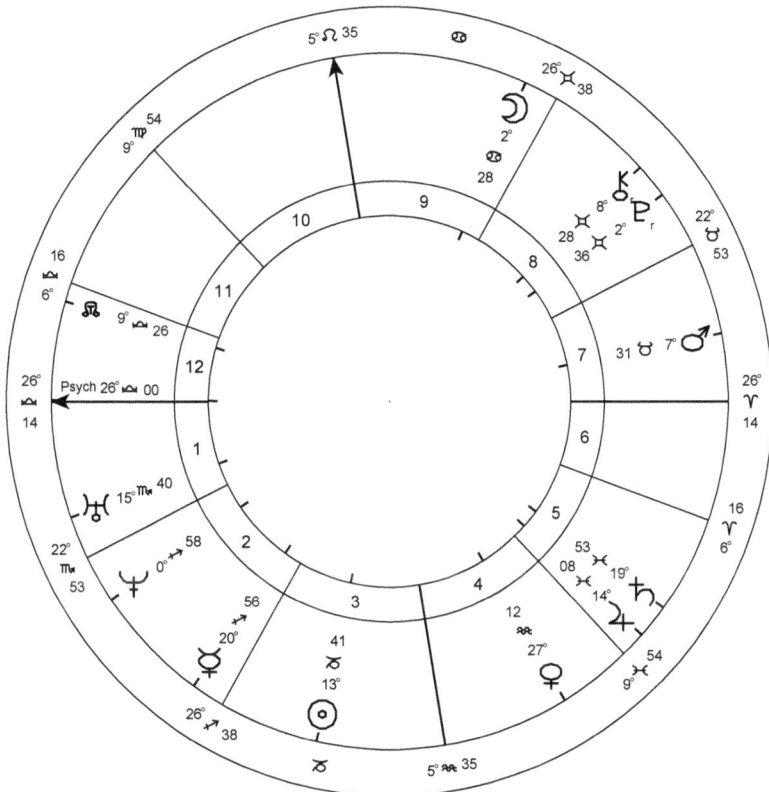

du Châtelet felt with Koenig: the painful bite of doubt about his scientific value, the need to question his competence. Their common experience at this time may be related to the fact they both had Venus in Aquarius, which indicates that they placed their sense of personal worth in their mastery of theoretical, mathematical, and astronomical knowledge. The work he then completed in three months was the seed of his masterpiece, the famous *Principia*, which occupied Émilie du Châtelet for so long.

In Newton's chart, Psyche is in Libra (perhaps on the ascendant, but his birth time is not certain), in close trine to Venus. The qualities of Libra, which can range from respect for equality in partnerships to a love of the beauty of the laws governing the universe, combine wonderfully with the values of Venus in Aquarius. The wisdom and perhaps the moderation of

Libra (Newton was known for overreacting and his gift for making enemies) were necessary if he were to enjoy the sense of personal worth Venus in Aquarius could offer him, along with her love of universal scientific knowledge. But the qualities of Libra needed a relationship to come into being. Thus, even for this inveterate loner, the trine between the progressed Sun and Psyche highlighted two relationships: one that ended with his only friend, whom he never saw again, and a more ephemeral one with Halley, which led him to question his scientific expertise, thanks to which he gained immortality through his *Principia*.

Gérard de Nerval

Gérard de Nerval was a French Romantic poet born under the name Gérard Labrunie at the beginning of the nineteenth century, in 1808. His birth chart is particularly interesting: the Sun and the Moon form close aspects to Psyche, a quincunx and an opposition respectively. Nerval never knew his mother, who left him when he was two weeks old to follow her husband, who'd enlisted in Napoleon's army. She entrusted him first to a nurse and then to his maternal great-uncle, and died two years later in Silesia. As for his father, he didn't meet him until he was seven, when he returned from the war. He lacked the most important relationships of his childhood, indeed of his life, and the aspects between the luminaries and Psyche reinforce the significance of this lack. (Aspects between Psyche and the luminaries will be discussed in Part Four.)

Nerval's progressed Sun made an exact trine to his natal Psyche in the third week of May 1838. We know that at this point in his life he suffered a heartbreak from which he never recovered, and which haunted him until his suicide in 1855. In 1834, Nerval met the actress and singer Jenny Colon, with whom he fell passionately in love. For months, he rented the same seat in the front row of the orchestra every night to watch her without making any attempt to approach her. After being introduced to her by a mutual friend, he tried in vain for a whole year to have an opera of *La Reine de Saba* performed for her, as she wanted to join an operatic stage. Finally, in October 1837, he was able to offer her some verses, which she sang in a comic opera. It's likely they became lovers soon after. At the end of February 1838, Victor Loubens, a friend, wrote: "Gérard writes in some newspapers and has been sleeping with Jenny Colon for three weeks: the great victory is finally achieved. He writes a lot of comic operas."[20]

---

20 Julie Anselmini, Claude Schopp. *Dumas amoureux* (Presses universitaires de Caen, 2020). https://doi.org/10.4000/books.puc.12077.

Unfortunately, this relationship was far from happy, as his friend Alexandre Dumas reported: "One morning I saw Gérard arrive, his eyes red with tears. It was the height of his passion. Jenny Colon, who cheated on him only three times a week, threatened to cheat on him every day. He was desperate in the face of this colonisation, but silent, because he loved her too much to accuse her."[21] This anecdote probably dates from February or March 1838, two months before the exact trine Then came tragedy, the tragedy of Nerval's life: on 11 April, Colon married a flautist from the comic opera company. The progressed Sun was then at 0°06 from the exact trine to Psyche. In *Aurelia*, which he wrote at the end of his life, Nerval recalled the event as follows: "Everyone can search his memory for the most painful emotion, the most terrible blow that fate has dealt to the soul; one must then decide to die or to live:- I'll explain later why I didn't choose death."[22] He threw himself headlong into travel and "vulgar intoxication." Jenny Colon died shortly afterwards, in 1842, which greatly disturbed him.

In Nerval's birth chart, Venus is in Taurus in the fifth house, in aspects to Saturn, Chiron and Pluto. This configuration suggests that love relationships are complex issues for him, very intense, serious and potentially painful. It may also have been difficult for him to appreciate himself and find beauty in himself. In his case, Psyche was in Scorpio, where there was also a stellium made up of Uranus, Saturn and the North Node. These four points in the chart counterbalance the other stellium, this time in Taurus, made up of the Moon, Venus, Mars, Mercury and the South Node. The sign of Taurus, quite strikingly, seems much more accessible to Nerval than Scorpio: the South Node is there, showing an innate or very early conditioned way of responding to the environment. What's more, the planets in Taurus are personal and extremely important. Even the Sun in Gemini probably struggled to express itself, at least at first. But the tension between Scorpio and Taurus must have been constant: Uranus in Scorpio opposes the Moon, and Saturn opposes Venus, Mars and Mercury. Of the wisdom of Scorpio, Nerval initially knew only Saturn, and the planet was more a source of fear, inadequacy and anguish in the face of intimacy than of self-knowledge. By falling in love with a woman to whom he didn't dare

---

21 Arsène Houssaye, *Confessions d'un demi-siècle. 1830-1880*, tome I (Paris, E. Dentu, 1885; BnF collection ebooks, 2015).
22 Gérard de Nerval, *Aurélia, Sylvie, Les chimères* (Libertalia 2018).

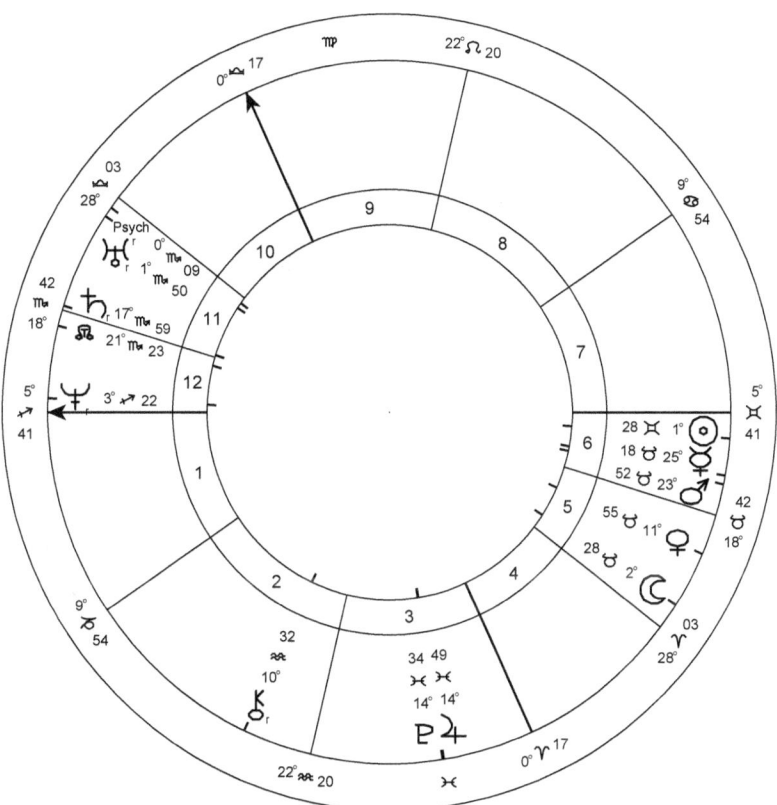

speak for more than two years, and then accepting that she was constantly cheating on him, Gérard de Nerval was in fact protecting himself from the dangers of an intimate relationship and shared love, according to the opposition of Venus to Saturn in Scorpio and Uranus to the Moon. When he met Psyche, Nerval finally lost Jenny Colon, whom he'd never really had. Psyche in Scorpio was then triggered, and the sign expressed itself differently than when it was Saturn. It urged him to take the risk of plunging into Hades, into the realm of his painful emotions and the emotional shortcomings of his childhood, in order to make healthier Venusian connections in the future. The choices Scorpio makes, its wisdom according to Plato, can't be separated from its courage to plunge into the dark, icy waters of its emotions. In the magnificent *Sylvie*, published almost twenty years later, Gérard de Nerval showed his vision of love after Jenny Colon. Marcel Proust wrote of this novella: "If there is a writer who is the antithesis of clear, simple watercolours, who laboriously kept seeking to define himself, to illuminate the murky nuances and profound laws of the almost elusive sensations of the human soul, it is Gérard de Nerval in Sylvie."[23] At the beginning of the story, the narrator goes to see an actress who has captivated him. When a friend tells him that she is already engaged, he greeted the news with indifference, as he had no intention of courting her. She reminds him of a former love, of whom he has no idea what has become of her since she entered the convent, and of another, Sylvie, whom he decides to seek out. The story ends with the narrator having understood the source of his obsessions and dreams, after an inner quest driven by these three women. He decides to abandon them, realising that his feelings of love weren't genuine. This is Scorpio, with its lucidity, its ability to question its motivations in depth, and also its courage, which can go so far as to renounce any union that's only desired through projections and in which the chosen person is not loved for herself.

Venus in the fifth house suggests that the cult of the goddess was linked to his creativity, which was fuelled by his search for the feminine ideal, lost as soon as it was glimpsed and for women who were deified and therefore unattainable. His suffering allowed him to nourish his writing, to go far in expressing the torments of the human soul. Writing as an artistic expression was truly an outlet for the difficult aspects of his Venus, which aspects Chiron, Saturn and Pluto. Psyche in Scorpio is also evident throughout his work, in its depth and subtlety, in the way he was able to portray the subterranean world of emotions. Nerval had Neptune rising, and Psyche may also have given him the clarity he needed to realise that he wasn't looking for a wife or a companion, but a goddess, a saviour, a redeemer.

Finally, it's worth noting that Nerval was influenced by Plato's philosophy in general, and also by the myth of Psyche, with both luminaries aspecting the asteroid. In *Aurelia,* written the year after the discovery of the asteroid, he wrote: "The Golden Ass of Apuleius, the Divine Comedy of

---

23 Marcel Proust, *Contre Sainte-Beuve* (Gallimard, coll. Bibliothèque de la Pléiade, 1971).

Dante, are the poetic models [for] studies of the human soul."[24] The search for his female Cupid was indeed one of the guiding principles of his life and the source of his inspiration. Unlike the other people mentioned in this book, he preferred Isis, like Lucius at the end of Apuleius' *Golden Ass* (or *Metamorphoses*), to a woman of flesh and blood, with whom he could have experienced *Voluptas*, the happiness that Apuleius said was intended for human beings.

---

24 Gérard de Nerval, *Aurélia, Sylvie, Les chimères* (Libertalia 2018).

Marie-Antoinette

As her progressed Sun opposed Psyche, Marie-Antoinette became aware of the hold one of King Louis XV's daughters (her aunts-in-law), had over her. She was in fact under her influence and had abandoned her judgement and the interests of her family to please her, for she needed her support and affection because of her isolation in France. The Dauphine's progressed Sun was exactly opposite Psyche from 5–10 January 1772. After arriving in France in 1770 for her wedding to the future Louis XVI, she'd been in constant correspondence with her mother, the Empress of Austria. As this marriage was the pledge of a new Franco-Austrian friendship, it had to be a success. Marie-Antoinette had to be accepted and then liked at the French court, and she had to start by pleasing the most important person in the kingdom – King Louis XV. Her mother repeated this to her in her letters, while at the same time telling the Austrian ambassador at Versailles, Mercy, that she hoped her daughter would gain some influence on the king.

Towards the end of his life, Louis XV took as his mistress a courtesan, the natural daughter of a dressmaker, Madame du Barry. The latter had alienated the king's daughters, aunts of the future Louis XVI, who couldn't bear to see their father indulge in such a public liaison. Madame Adelaide, the eldest of Louis XV's living daughters, was the most dreadful. Having already nicknamed the previous royal favourite, Madame de Pompadour (Madame Hooker), she'd naturally directed her contempt and intrigues against Jeanne du Barry, dragging her sisters Sophie and Victoire, who remained at Versailles, in her wake. On her arrival in France, Marie-Antoinette was advised by her mother to be kind to her aunts: not only were they the daughters of the current King of France, but Madame Adelaide was also very close to the future King. In fact, she had a certain influence on her nephew Louis-Auguste, the future Louis XVI. Having lost his father and mother, he thought that Adelaide, who'd been very close to his father, was his posthumous voice. Her salon, in particular, was known as a place where reputations were made, and Marie-Antoinette had to look after her own. Louis XV's daughters were delighted to spend time with the archduchess and to introduce her to their salon. They were thus able to add not only the future King but also his wife, the Dauphine, to Jeanne du Barry's list of enemies.

Naively, Marie-Antoinette thought she was doing the right thing by getting closer to her in-laws, for her friendship with Madame Adelaide was at least one thing she shared with her husband, with whom she found it so difficult to connect. Moreover, having been rather isolated when she first arrived, she felt accepted by her new family. After all, as the daughter of an empress, she thought it was normal to associate only with the daughters of kings. Jeanne du Barry's place at Louis XV's side offended her. The daughters of Louis XV and Marie-Antoinette agreed to ignore the old king's mistress. At the end of December 1770, the Dauphine's disdain was exacerbated by the dismissal of the minister who had favoured the Austrian marriage. He was replaced by an intimate of the favourite. Marie-Antoinette's reaction was to declare war on the mistress: she wouldn't say a word to her anymore. For months she didn't speak to the King's mistress. According to the rules of the French court, Jeanne du Barry wasn't allowed to initiate conversation with a royal: an icy silence fell between the two women, and soon between the Dauphine and the entire entourage of the favourite.

This was too humiliating for the King's mistress and she complained to her lover. Louis XV addressed the matter by asking the Austrian ambassador to speak to his daughter-in-law, but he was unable to persuade the Dauphine to comply. The Empress of Austria, informed by her ambassador Mercy, was well aware that her daughter was in Adelaide's power. After all, the Dauphine was just over sixteen at the time, while Adelaide was thirty-nine! Marie-Antoinette thought she knew and understood everything, but she was merely a pawn in political intrigues and court quarrels. By alienating Madame du Barry, she was alienating the King and working against her Austrian family; but she hardly realised it, spending her time spreading slander with Adelaide and her sisters. The Empress of Austria had to urge her daughter in numerous letters to please the King of France. In her own country, the Empress had prostitutes whipped and sent to reformatories, and her daughter knew it. But in France, the King did as he pleased, and Marie-Antoinette had to obey him. The tug-of-war went on for seven months. In August 1771, five months before the exact opposition to Psyche, she began to point the finger of blame at her aunts in general and Madame Adelaide in particular. Not only was her daughter stubbornly refusing to speak to Jeanne du Barry, but she was also beginning to show condescension towards others: "This is attributed to Mesdames who have never been able to win the esteem and trust of others", the Empress wrote.[25] A month later, she felt obliged to increase the pressure on her daughter, who was persisting in her behaviour: "You only act through your aunts [...] You have therefore allowed yourself to be led into such slavery that reason and even your duty no longer have the power to persuade you."

Marie-Antoinette seemed to be under Adelaide's influence, losing all judgement, like Psyche who accepts not knowing who her husband is. In Marie-Antoinette's chart, Venus is in the fifth house, closely conjunct the Sun. This conjunction suggests that Marie-Antoinette's sense of identity was closely linked to the expression of Venus. Like the Sun, Venus is in Scorpio, highlighting the relationship issues specific to this sign, particularly the problem of power struggles. In whose hands had she left her personal power? Venus is also almost exactly square Neptune, suggesting that Marie-Antoinette may have trusted her relatives too easily due to a degree of idealism and lack of judgement.

Her mother was no fool. Speaking of Louis XV, she reminded Marie-Antoinette: "You are his first subject, you owe him obedience and submission", Marie-Antoinette behaved undutifully, "through a shameful complacency for people who have subjugated you by treating you like a child." Venus in Scorpio can't be honoured when someone is under such an influence. This Venus, in order to bring joy and self-esteem, must be able to see beyond the surface, to feel what's hidden, and to make deep and intense connections. For the very young Marie-Antoinette, this was clearly not yet the case. Her mother concluded her September letter: "I see you in great submission", and she added something that would make a Scorpio shudder: "Excessive complacency is baseness or weakness." The power struggle continued, but this time between Marie-Antoinette and her mother: the latter, after using an authoritarian and pressing tone, then tried emotional blackmail: "But what angered me and convinced me of your unwillingness

---

25 Evelyne Lever, *Marie-Antoinette, Correspondance, 1770-1793* (Tallandier 2006).

Marie-Antoinette

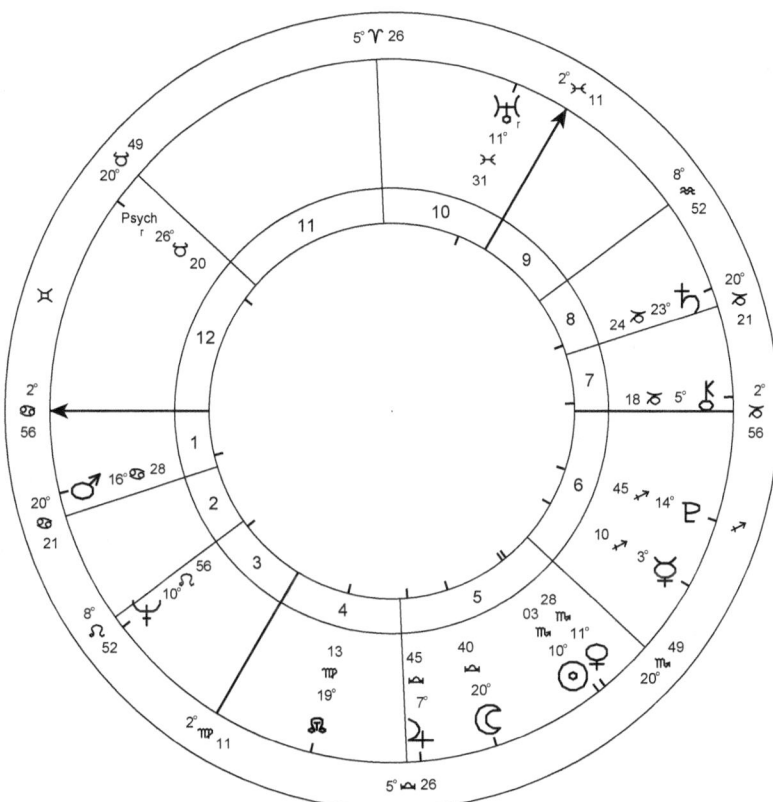

to correct yourself was your total silence on the subject of your aunts [...] Is my advice, my tenderness, less worthy of return than theirs? I confess it breaks my heart." With the progressed Sun at 0°20 from the exact opposition to Psyche, Marie-Antoinette was caught in a vice between two people to whom she was very close, both trying to manipulate her. Her mother undoubtedly loved her, which was probably not the case with Madame Adelaide, but she used her daughter for diplomatic purposes and tried to influence her, mainly to further Austrian policy in Europe.

In the chart of the future Queen of France, Psyche is in Taurus and in the twelfth house. At the end of 1771 and the beginning of 1772, this Scorpio woman was under the double influence of Madame Adelaide and her mother. Taurus may have a reputation for stubbornness, but this is sometimes a good quality: in any case, it was one that Marie-Antoinette had to develop in order to form her own opinions and not change them at the whim of those who wished to use her for their own ends. The situation in which the Dauphine found herself evoked the Platonic virtues of wisdom and justice, for she had to make up her mind, to separate the wishes of others from her own and her own interests, and to understand for herself whether she had to please her husband, who was attached to his aunts, or the King of France, the ruler of her new homeland, or her mother and the interests of her country of birth. In other words, she had to define her values, the importance of which is underlined by the position of Psyche in Taurus. When we think of this sign, we may have an image of a rooted animal, difficult to move against its will: Marie-Antoinette needed this quality to avoid becoming a weathervane, yielding to the most persuasive. In the zodiac, Taurus and Scorpio are opposite but complementary. This intense, passionate Venus, ready to burst into flames and take up the cause of those she loved, needed the more concrete, realistic approach of Taurus. Both are faithful and loyal signs, and Marie-Antoinette must have felt terribly torn between her loyalty to her mother and her loyalty to her rank and the people who seemed to have taken her in. But Taurus can teach Scorpio a taste for serenity, for temporary withdrawal if necessary for peace, and the ability to resist unwanted influences. Marie-Antoinette's Venus in Scorpio was later expressed in her affair with Count Axel de Fersen, but her Psyche in Taurus initially led her to choose a simpler life, sheltered from intrigue, in her Petit Trianon and Hameau, where she had a farm and a country village built. There she also enjoyed the pleasures of the theatre. But in 1772, at the time of the exact opposition to Psyche, she wasn't yet ready to reveal the qualities of Taurus: instead of giving in to Adelaide, she gave in to the King, to Du Barry and to her mother.

Thus, during the ceremonies of 1 January 1772, the long-awaited words were spoken. On that day, the opposition between the progressed Sun and Psyche was almost exact, with an orb of 0°01. To Jeanne Du Barry, but in the midst of a large crowd, Marie-Antoinette uttered the famous phrase: "Today there is a great crowd at Versailles."[26] And that was that: the Dauphine could no longer be blamed for anything, but she was determined

---

26 John Hardmann, *Marie-Antoinette : The Making of a French Queen* (Yale University Press, 2019).

to make no further effort. Surrender had cost her more than anyone could imagine. She quickly told her ambassador, Mercy: "I spoke to her once, but that woman will never hear the sound of my voice again." The aunts continued to ignore Du Barry. And, according to Mercy, the confrontation between Adelaide and Marie-Antoinette was stormy.

Gradually, after this episode, she managed to distance herself sufficiently from her aunts' intrigues. Thus, in June, five months after the exact opposition Mercy was able to report to the Empress with satisfaction: "Although the influence of Mesdames is still operative in many circumstances, it is not so effective as to have dangerous effects."[27] She began to spend more time with her husband's brother and his wife, without the aunts. Eventually she only saw them out of courtesy. As her progressed Sun shone on Psyche, Marie-Antoinette probably learned a lot about herself and others. It opened her eyes to court intrigue, power struggles, hypocrisy (including that of her mother, who had prostitutes whipped in her empire), and the pretence that drives behaviour. In other words, she came to know the qualities of Venus in Scorpio and stopped getting involved with people indiscriminately. It was Madame Adelaide who later gave Marie-Antoinette the nickname "Austrian", which did her considerable harm. She was the source of many rumours and gathered her enemies in her castle. As for Marie-Antoinette, she was never as naive as she'd been before her encounter with Psyche. Unfortunately, her refusal to be used and her avoidance of court intrigue led her to retreat more than she should have into her Petit Trianon and her theatre plays, contributing towards the dark legend of a queen unconcerned with her duties and her people.

---

27 Evelyne Lever, *Marie-Antoinette, Correspondance, 1770-1793* (Tallandier 2006).

Maria Montessori

Maria Montessori's progressed Sun made an exact trine to her natal Psyche at the end of November 1897, when she was twenty-seven years old. She'd discovered shortly before that she was pregnant. At that time, Montessori had only been a doctor for a year and was working at the Psychiatric Clinic of the University of Rome in collaboration with Giuseppe Montesano. She'd studied medicine against the advice of her father, but with the support of her mother. Montessori had faced many problems, mostly related to the misogyny of the time, and had given private lessons to pay part of her school fees. She worked at night to practise dissection, as it was unthinkable for a woman of her time to see naked male bodies. She was the third Italian woman to obtain a degree in medicine. Montessori was ambitious and determined: what she saw in the psychiatric clinic, where mentally handicapped children were mixed with adults, convinced her to spend her first years as a doctor trying to make their lives easier. The many successes she had with the so-called "idiots" led her to develop her own pedagogy for normal children.

In 1897, Montessori was the mistress of Giuseppe Montesano, with whom she worked. Their affair was secret. When she discovered she was pregnant, sometime between September and November 1897, her world fell apart: in Italy it was unthinkable for a married woman to continue working. Her husband's permission was required by law, but worse still, no one would have trusted a woman who was supposed to take care of her husband and children. On the other hand, being a single mother would have tarnished her reputation, and a female doctor was supposed to embody a kind of bourgeois ideal of good behaviour. Montessori never really talked about these dark hours of her life, but her son did get some information that he passed on to his descendants. One of them, Carolina Montessori, wrote a book.[28] According to her, it was Maria's mother, Renilde Montessori, who

---

28 Maria Montessori, *Maria Montessori Sails to America*, translated and introduced by Carolina Montessori (Montessori-Pierson Publishing Company, 2013).

guided her daughter in the middle of her pregnancy, when the progressed Sun was trine Psyche. Renilde met Giuseppe Montesano's parents, who also wanted to avoid any scandal that could harm their son's carrier. Both families agreed to conceal Maria's pregnancy and birth.[29] Maria's mother made everyone believe that her daughter was travelling so she could end her pregnancy discreetly. She gave birth to her son at home on 31 March 1898. Then it was time for Maria to make the most difficult decision of her life: a midwife registered the child at birth, informing the registry office that he was born of an unknown mother and father. She entrusted him to farmers who lived 45 kilometres from Rome. He was given the name Mario and the invented surname Pipilli.

In Montessori's birth chart, Venus is in Leo. This sign's relationship with children is well known, as is its love of play. Montessori dedicated her life to children and used their natural inclination to play as a means of achieving their educational goals. Leo is the sign where what has been built up in the first five signs, one's identity, can shine; it's where one becomes the king of one's kingdom, like the lion in the savannah, or like Apollo, the Sun god crowned by his golden hair, to become the centre of one's own solar system. Venus in Leo therefore played an important role in Montessori's thinking. This is reflected in her position conjunct the ascendant, from the twelfth house, in the Gauquelin sector. Any planet conjunct the ascendant serves as a psychic guide because she was rising in the East, the Orient, at birth. Orientation comes from the verb "orient", so Venus is a planet that should orient Maria. But it's in the twelfth house, which gives her a universal colour, the ability to love and welcome children unconditionally, and to find value in all of them. Given this important connection between Maria and children, she could reasonably have chosen to care for her own child and give up her career. However, Venus in the twelfth house connected her to something greater than herself and made her hear a call to give up the ego and serve an ideal or alleviate human suffering. Maria made a very painful but clear choice: she would serve all children, not just her own. Once again, we see that the encounter with Psyche can be a difficult time: Lennon was sued by McCartney, Nietzsche had to lose Wagner to be true to his thinking, and Marie-Antoinette had to give up her pride. Montessori, to be true to her Venus in the twelfth house, had to give up her child and her relationship with her lover.

---

29 Cristina de Stefano, *The Child is The Teacher* (Other Press, 2022).

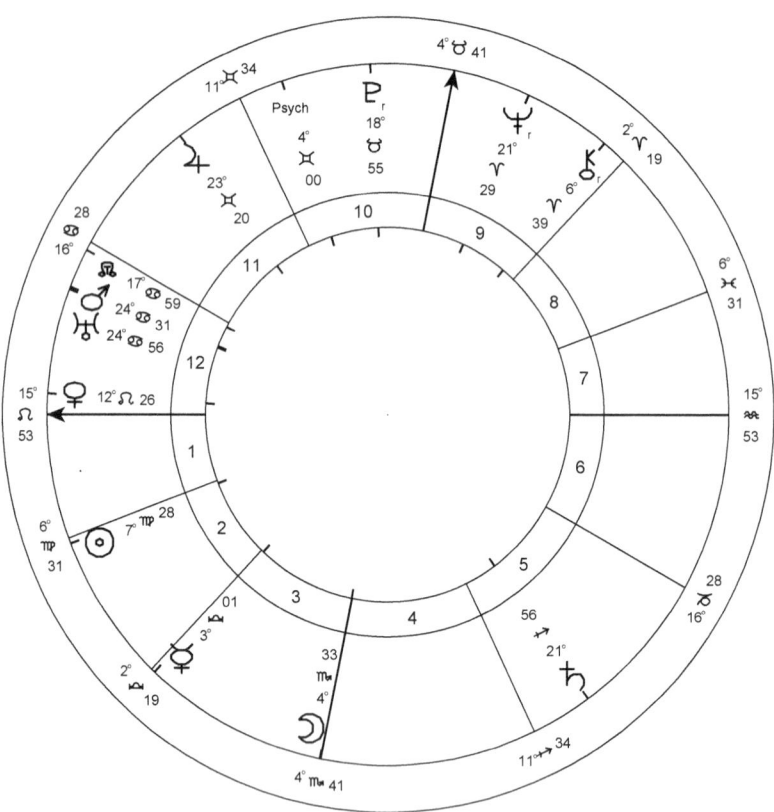

This universal Venus needed Psyche's qualities at the time of Montessori's pregnancy: in her case, the asteroid is at 4° Gemini, trine Mercury in Libra, quincunx the Moon in Scorpio at the IC, and square the Sun in Virgo. Venus disposes of Mercury, and Mercury disposes of Psyche and the Sun. The Moon in Scorpio appears isolated, and the myth of Kore and Persephone who had to renounce each other comes to the fore. Psyche in Gemini helped Maria make her decision not on the basis of her desire or lack of desire for motherhood, nor on the basis of the role assigned to women in Italy at the time, but according to her opinion, and vocation, considering her aspects to Mercury and the Sun. Gemini is the democrat of the zodiac because it's convinced that everyone has the right to decide for themselves and make up their own minds. What's more, Psyche in an air sign, as well as Mercury, her ruler, in Libra, emphasise the importance for Montessori of the qualities of her intellect and of retaining a certain amount of freedom to be able to exercise them. During her pregnancy, transiting Saturn in Sagittarius was squaring the Sun: Maria was called upon to take responsibility, make choices and define herself as an individual. The activation of Psyche at this time shows that the choices had to be made in relation to Venus, and through the unveiling of Gemini's qualities. She certainly needed the virtues of courage and justice, in order to play her role, to do what she was gifted at and felt called to do, ignoring society's expectations for a woman. Like Psyche in the myth, she descended deeply into the realm of Proserpine, and part of her, the mother, died there.

The decision she made in the middle of her pregnancy cost her another relationship: with Montesano. In fact, they ended their love affair at the same time. Carolina Montessori explains in her book: "What exactly happened is quite mysterious. Probably Giuseppe Montesano agreed not to marry Maria and to look after the child from a distance, hoping to marry her later. When he realised this wasn't going to happen, it damaged their relationship."[30] On 29 September 1901, Giuseppe legally recognised his son, but left him in the care of his foster parents. Urged by his family to marry a woman and respect the traditions, he got engaged and married a woman called Maria Aprile on 6 October. Maria ended her collaboration with him and gave up her beloved work at the psychiatric clinic. According to Carolina Montessori, she cried for days.

For Montessori, the encounter with Psyche led to the end of her relationship with her lover. Her relationship with her son didn't have a chance to develop and it died at the same time as it began. Through these relationships, Montessori had to find out what she really wanted, who she would follow. Would she marry Giuseppe and live the traditional bourgeois life of a housewife? Or would she have to sacrifice part of herself, follow her mother's advice and abandon her child? Venus demands that we choose our values and act them out in the world. The activation of Psyche by the progressed Sun guided her decision by revealing some of the Gemini qualities necessary for a healthy expression of Venus. This sign can show great courage in the name of freedom, and its sense of justice, in the Platonic

---

30 Maria Montessori, *Maria Montessori Sails to America*, translated and introduced by Carolina Montessori (Montessori-Pierson Publishing Company, 2013).

sense of the term, couldn't be satisfied with a sense of belonging born of conformity to a social role. Because he feared confinement, especially on an intellectual level, Gemini gave her the wisdom not to act out of guilt but to look ahead. And indeed Montessori couldn't put herself in the position of serving only her own child. Her twelfth house Venus served as a guide and a force for the mission that the close aspects of Chiron to the two luminaries entrusted to her: to give herself to the wounded, to those whose abnormality or monstruosity, like the centaur, was deemed intolerable. She would later extend the scope of her insights to normal children, also embodying Chiron, the teacher and foster parent. The labours required by Venus were extremely cruel for Maria, who had to give up her lover and her son. But this was the price she had to pay to follow her path, to live her Sun and to claim immortality. At the beginning of the twenty-first century, there were 25,000 Montessori schools worldwide. She was finally able to meet her son Mario when he was a teenager, at a time when her reputation was strong and her work well advanced. They developed a very harmonious relationship, and he ended up working and travelling with her.

Jeanne

One of my clients, Jeanne, was also pregnant when her progressed Sun hit Psyche, but she lost her child. This devastating loss caused her to break up with her sister, with whom she had an important relationship. When they were children, Jeanne, her sister Elisabeth and their mother formed a close family, while their father, who was elsewhere and periodically trying to start a new life, was insignificant. As the older child, she felt obliged to help her mother and looked after her younger sister as best she could. She even played the role of surrogate mother when she was left alone with her sister when they were sixteen and eleven years old respectively. Their mother had to go to Paris to look for work, leaving them at home, the older to look after the younger, who was still in secondary school.

In adulthood, the relationship between the two sisters remained intense, to the extent that the eldest's successive boyfriends had accused her of putting her relationship with her sister above all others. It was an unbalanced relationship, and the younger sister understood that her older sister never refused her anything. She was used to taking full advantage of that. In Jeanne's chart, Venus in Taurus is quincunx Uranus and square Jupiter. It's clear from what she told me that she had experienced the faithful and tenacious aspect of Taurus and projected Uranus and Jupiter onto her lovers. Jeanne became pregnant just after the quincunx between the progressed Sun and Psyche. It seems that her decision to have a child was a way of putting her sister away, daring for the first time in her life to put another being before her sister. Sadly, she lost the baby two months later. Although she'd been informed of the miscarriage, two days later her sister emailed her a photo of her own ultrasound scan, without a word, her way of telling her she was pregnant.

This was far more than Jeanne could bear, and when she became pregnant again a few weeks later, she decided not to see or speak to her sister for the duration of her pregnancy. This decision was made just before the progressed Sun was half a degree past the exact quincunx to

Psyche. In her chart the asteroid is in Scorpio, exactly opposite Venus. This Taurus-Scorpio combination has already been discussed as it appears in Marie-Antoinette's chart: the qualities of the two signs are complementary rather than opposite, as they can relate to each other through the intensity of their feelings and their loyalty. But Scorpio senses things Taurus would prefer to ignore, and Jeanne benefited from the wisdom of Scorpio, which can see where a relationship is unhealthy and damaging to the individual. Cutting herself off from her sister for a few years allowed her to quietly play the role of Demeter with her daughter – suggested by her Moon, Sun and Venus in Taurus – without being disturbed by the sacrifices she was making for her sister. She rediscovered the simple, peaceful life so cherished by Taurus. And when they were in touch again, she kept her distance in the relationship, leaving space for the quincunx of Uranus to Venus.

Marcel Proust

The most painful event in the life of the French writer Marcel Proust occurred when his progressed Sun was coming up to form a semi-sextile to Psyche. It was the death of his mother (at that moment the orb of the semi-sextile was of 0°26): "She took my life with her, just as Papa had taken hers",[31] he wrote shortly afterwards. Two months later, at his mother's insistence, Proust agreed to spend six weeks in hospital to cure his "neurasthenia". The death of his mother and his hospitalisation, less than six months before the exact semi-sextile, are among the elements that need to be examined in order to understand what was at stake for Proust at this time.

Proust was born into a family of doctors. His brother Robert was an oncologist and urologist, and his father Adrien was a hygienist. Marcel's health was fragile. From the age of nine, he suffered from debilitating asthma which, although it left him in peace for a few years, returned when he was twenty-three. He was poly-allergic and suffered from what today would be called chronic fatigue or anxiety and depression, depending on the aetiology. For a man like Adrien Proust, an advocate of fresh air and physical exercise, it was difficult to have a fragile son who shunned outdoor air as a trigger for allergies. For him, his son was neurasthenic. The relationship between father and son was complicated by a lack of mutual understanding. In 1897, Adrien Proust even co-wrote a book entitled *Hygiene for the Neurasthenic*, in which the authors argued that neurasthenia was linked to intellectual overwork, combined with a thirst for achievement or success, in other words, ambition. They highlighted the frequent association of neurasthenia with respiratory problems. To prevent the development of neurasthenia in susceptible individuals, they recommended daily exercise and regular rest. A person's social life was also mentioned as an aggravating factor. When reading this treatise on hygiene, one can't help but recognise the life of his son Marcel.

---

31 Marcel Proust, *Correspondance de Marcel Proust, tome V* (Plon. 1979, p.345).

Proust's mother had probably been convinced by her husband of the nervous origin of her son's respiratory problems. Before she died, she made him promise to treat his neurasthenia. Devastated by her death, he kept his promise and began a six-week course of treatment at the clinic of psychiatrist Paul Sollier in Boulogne-sur-Seine. When he entered the clinic, the progressed Sun was 0°12 from the semi-sextile to Psyche; when he left, the progressed Sun was 0°04 from it. Paul Sollier proposed using hypnosis to provoke revivifications in order to discover a repressed trauma. Proust returned to Paris on 25 January 1906, suffering terribly from asthma and more ill than when he'd left. After this episode, he continued to doubt the efficacy of psychotherapy and never tried it again. For Proust, this encounter with Psyche involved the death of his mother, the event that triggered his entry into psychotherapy, and a relationship with Paul Sollier that we can only assume was complicated. For eight weeks, Sollier tried to help him rediscover repressed traumas. This therapy is reminiscent of the primal therapy John Lennon underwent, also at the time of a meeting between the progressed Sun and Psyche.

In Proust's chart, Psyche is in Cancer in the fourth house: this therapy certainly had the effect of allowing Proust to question his childhood and to make contact with his inner child. Unveiling the qualities of Cancer in him meant taking into account the unique individual he was, and taking care of the fragile child within him, recognising him and giving him a place. Proust was confronted with the memories of his childhood, and this may have been the seed for the writing of *In Search of Lost Time* a few months later. The therapy didn't have the desired effect: forcing Proust to relive his memories made him physically ill for months and led him to protect himself more and more from the outside world.

In the following months, Proust wrote many times about his mother's death. It was, as he said, the trauma of his life. But in the background, the death of his father also came to the surface. Neptune, then in Cancer, went back and forth over Proust's IC, symbolising his foundations, his home and, for many astrologers, his father. The intense relationship between Marcel and his mother is well known, but Proust's stellium in Cancer, composed of Jupiter, Mercury, the Sun, Uranus (and Psyche) is located in the fourth house, and the cusp of the house is also in Cancer. This father, who always seemed partly inaccessible to him (Uranus is in the stellium), did everything he could to ensure his son's health and comfort, even if he

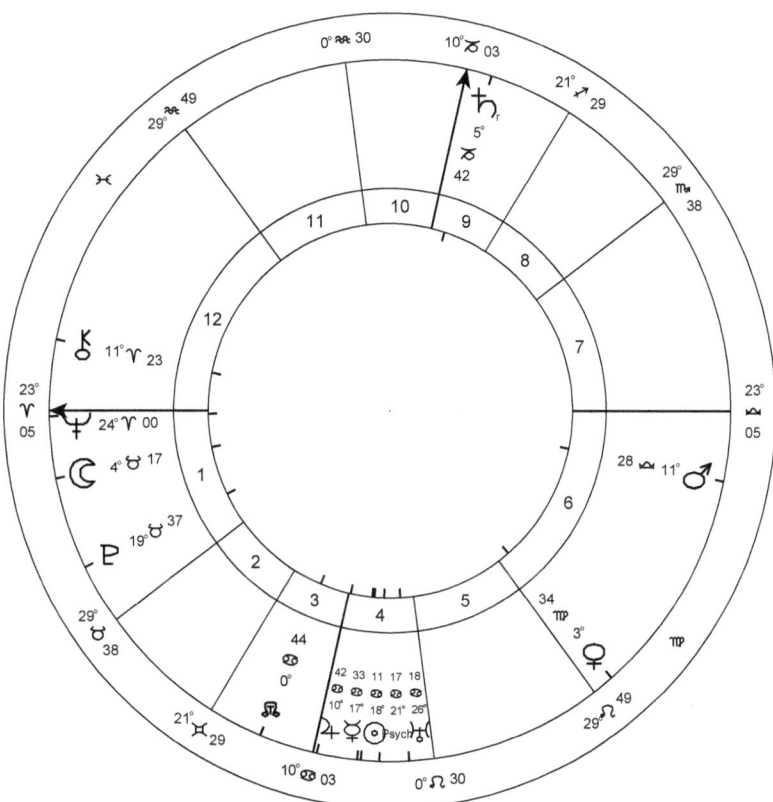

didn't approve his life's choices. He'd allowed Marcel to live the life he'd chosen, paying for his clothes, his orchids, his gifts, his dinners and his twelve-hour rides in hired cars. Added to this were bills of several hundred francs a month for the treatments Proust chose to try for his asthma, insomnia, rheumatism and indigestion. So there's more here than the distant father, we can feel that the good and supportive father was just in the background, with Jupiter also in the Cancerian stellium. In *In Search of Lost Time*, Proust wrote of the narrator's father: "Was coldness only an external aspect of my father's sensitivity? For it is perhaps the human truth of this double aspect: [...] when people used to say of my father: "Beneath his icy coldness, he hides an extraordinary sensitivity"; what he had above all was the modesty of his sensitivity." Here we find Cancer lurking in the background. Psyche is also there, and Proust's progressed Sun conjoined the asteroid when he was around the age of three. Unfortunately, we know nothing about what happened to him at this time, but as the conjunction occurred in the fourth house, it's possible his relationship with his father was already at stake.

Through Dr Sollier, Proust was confronted with the wishes of his parents. What did they want? That he would be stronger, that he would recover, that he would change his way of life by curing his depression. But what was Marcel's wish? Here's what one of his characters, a doctor, says about nervous people, who for him are the only true artistic or literary creators:

> Put up with being called a nervous girl. You belong to that wonderful and wretched family that is the salt of the earth. All the great things we know come to us from the nervous. It is they, not others, who have founded religions and composed masterpieces. The world will never know how much it owes them, and especially how much they suffered to give it. We enjoy fine music, beautiful paintings and a thousand delicacies, but we don't know what they cost those who invented them in sleeplessness, tears, convulsive laughter, hives, asthma, epilepsy and a fear of dying worse than all these.[32]

The six weeks in the sanatorium had the opposite effect to that hoped for by Proust's parents. Thanks to Proust's correspondence, we know 1906 was a time when his health was at its worst. In June 1906, he confided to his mother's doctor that he hadn't left his bed for six months. In fact, he only made one or two attempts, and just when he seemed to be getting better, he came down with influenza, which kept him bedridden for several weeks. After this episode he had fifteen years to live, most of which he spent confined to his house, lining his bedroom with cork to keep out the outside air. His servants disinfected the mail with formaldehyde. Instead of the fresh air and exercise advocated by Adrien Proust, Marcel resigned himself to a life of confinement.

In his chart, Venus is in the sixth house, in Virgo, and as we've already seen in the examples of Nietzsche and Lennon, it's very important for

---

32 Marcel Proust, *In Search of Lost Time* (Everyman, 2001).

such a Venus not to be polluted by the influence of the other. The father can be a pervasive and partly unconscious source of influence when the Sun is in the fourth house. Venus is also almost exactly trine the Moon, which is perfectly illustrated by a phrase like "I only love one person in this world, and that's Mum", and which creates another source of influence. The ascendant is in Aries, suggesting that Proust's taste for risk and the sign's ability to leave behind what makes it feel secure should serve as his psychic guide. But Neptune conjoins the ascendant, and Mars, the ruler of the chart, is exactly opposite Chiron. These aspects make Aries's assertiveness much more difficult to express, and can create a sense of impotence or chronic incapacity. What's more, as we saw earlier, Proust's chart contains a stellium of four planets in Cancer in the fourth house: the lunar issues are particularly emphasised by this configuration, including the issue of separation from the mother, and can complicate the Martian expression required by the Aries ascendant. However, Venus in Virgo clearly indicated that Marcel's values had to be freed from the influence of his parents.

After his release from the sanatorium, and while his progressed Sun was still under the influence of Psyche, Proust seemed to be getting worse and worse, and above all to be experiencing more and more grief, accompanied by more and more guilt. At the beginning of June, he wrote: "The way my grief has changed in the last few months is frightening, and it's now so much more painful."[33] And later, also in June: "I am too constantly worried that, with my poor health, I have only ever caused my parents grief, that I have always made their lives miserable." Proust thus seemed, at least unconsciously, stubborn: no, he wouldn't cure his neurasthenia, no, he wouldn't live in the fresh air and take exercise, and no, he wouldn't slow down his intellectual work or refrain from his literary work. We must remember that it's Venus who gives meaning to what we experience when we meet the asteroid. In Virgo, like the ant in the myth, she demands that Proust separate his values from those of his parents. Venus is in close trine to the Moon and in the sixth house, which evokes work and the mundane aspects of life, and therefore writing in Proust's case. This house is also traditionally associated with health. Is this the origin of Proust's admiration for the "nervous girl", the fact that he found great beauty in nervous illness? It was during this period of grief and physical suffering

---

33 Lettre à Ladilslas Landowski, a little after 8 June 1906.

that the first drafts of *In Search of Lost Time* were born. It's easy to see how a Venus in the sixth house trine the Moon could be satisfied with such a work, which revisits the childhood and family clan of a narrator whose life is little different from Proust's. This work also illustrates magnificently the talents and twists of mind produced by a stellium in Cancer in the fourth house. This stellium seems to have come into its own in terms of creativity only after the activation of Psyche in Cancer in early 1906. By agreeing to be the neurasthenic that his father was so keen to cure, and who, what's more, refused to accept his mother's grief and allowed himself to be overwhelmed by guilt, Proust had put the discernment of his Venus in Virgo to work. This planet finds her pleasure not in conforming to the wishes of others, but in making us choose what's desirable in our own eyes. Proust seemed to think inspiration came at a price: neurasthenia, asthma, confinement, the impossible mourning of his mother, guilt. His father would certainly have been very sorry. But, as the doctor quoted above put it, for him they were all creative forces. And, as he himself expressed it so well: "Real life, life finally uncovered, the only life in consequence lived to the full, is literature".[34]

---

[34] Marcel Proust, *Time Regained. In Search of Lost Time Vol. VI* (Modern Library 2003).

Robert Francis Kennedy

Born eight years after his brother John Fitzgerald, the future President of the United States, Robert was an incredibly effective ally in JFK's rise to power. But unlike his older brothers Joe Junior and John, he was never seen by his father Joe as a potential leader. He'd been brought up not to rule but to help, and that's what he did, right up until JFK's death. After his brother's assassination in November 1963, Robert resigned as attorney general and kept his distance from power, remaining only a senator. Then his progressed Sun met Psyche. As his biographer, Evan Thomas, states: "It took a series of setbacks in the late fall of 1966 and early winter of 1967 to shake him from his moody caution. For Robert Kennedy, the path to enlightenment always began in the darkest part of the forest. He needed to suffer before he could experience exaltation."[35] The last two sentences would apply to many people with an emphasis in Scorpio, like Robert, who had the Sun, Saturn and Mars in this sign. But this transformation needed Psyche to happen. It led to his decision to run for President in the 1968 US election.

In Robert's birth chart, Psyche is at 9°45 Gemini, less than 2 degrees from his brother John's Sun, as will be discussed in Part Four. Robert's progressed Sun made an exact quincunx to Psyche from 23–28 December 1966. As said earlier, the myth of Psyche begins with an offence to Venus, whose worship is halted. In Robert's chart, Venus is in Capricorn, conjunct Jupiter and the midheaven in the ninth house. She opposes Pluto in the third house, the house of siblings. Venus is the bringer of self-worth, and Robert, whose nickname was Bobby, notoriously struggled with low self-esteem. He was also sometimes nicknamed "Richelieu" after the minister to the French King Louis XIII who made most of the decisions but was sometimes overshadowed. He was in fact the *éminence grise* of his brother. However, the opposition between Venus conjunct the midheaven (the

---

35 Evan Thomas, *Robert Kennedy: his life* (Simon & Schuster 2002).

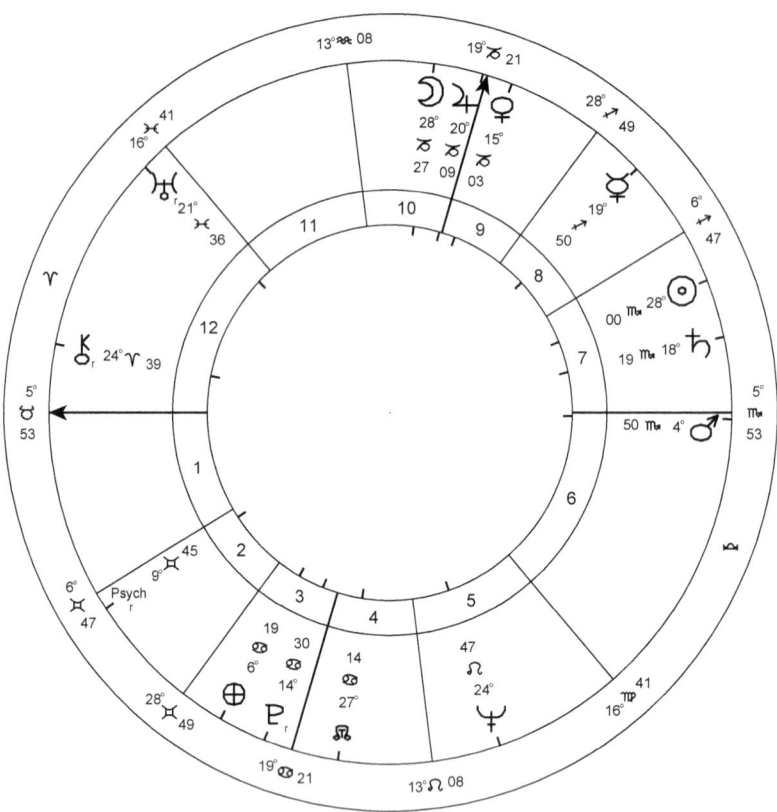

career and social image) and Pluto suggests he could find his worth by accepting the responsibility of power and identifying with the role of the beloved leader (Venus-Jupiter in Capricorn on the midheaven). The events of late 1966 and early 1967 seem to have been about the balance of power in his relationships. Was he asserting his opinions, views, and ambitions, or was he letting others have the power? The Venus-Pluto opposition is particularly significant in this regard. In addition, Robert has an emphasis in Scorpio, a sign in which interpersonal issues are of paramount importance for self-construction and self-discovery.

The first person to take power from Bobby in 1966 was his sister-in-law Jacqueline Kennedy, John's widow. Robert had probably been the only one to fully understand her after her husband's assassination, and they shared their grief. Robert had become the legal guardian of his brother's two children, so he did his best to be at Jackie's for breakfast and dinner, despite having eight children of his own. They finally became lovers in 1964 or 1965. They were two broken people who were just looking for a way to find comfort and they were truly attached to each other. But because of this attachment and his innate loyalty, Bobby's public image was about to be tarnished in early 1967, at least in the eyes of the electorate, by Jackie's whims and abuse of power. She'd decided, shortly after her husband's death, to give her account of JFK's last days to William Manchester, in an attempt to control what was said about him and avoid a sensational treatment of his assassination. Manchester had already written a book about Kennedy, *Portrait of a President* (1962), before his assassination, and his admiration for JFK was palpable. Both John and Jackie had enjoyed the book. Manchester then began work on *The Death of a President*, doing extensive research that proved exhausting. He finished the book while in hospital. In addition to Jackie and Bobby, he interviewed over a thousand people. Unwisely, he'd agreed to give the Kennedys final control over the manuscript, so in March 1966, Manchester sent his manuscript to Robert and Jackie and waited for their comments. Neither of them had the strength to read it. Robert gave it to some relatives who asked for only minor changes. These were accepted and on 29 July 1966, Robert Kennedy gave his official approval for the book to be published.

But Jackie, who had just returned from holiday and was told of Bobby's decision, panicked. She felt she'd given away too much personal information, and she didn't want her husband's murder to continue to make headlines. She complained to Robert. Bobby knew it was Jackie who'd chosen Manchester and he himself had given his blessing to the publication of the book that wouldn't tarnish his brother's reputation. But following his heart and not his head, he stood by Jackie. He shared her views as well as her grief. In August, he warned Manchester that he'd eventually refuse publication. In September, he supported the many changes Jackie's relatives wanted, and began to harass Manchester, chasing him into his bedroom in November, while the journalist, exhausted and ill, had checked into a hostel under a false name in order to leave for London.

Finally, Jackie, who was accustomed to getting what she wanted, made a fatal mistake for her and Bobby: she sued Manchester and *Look*, the magazine in which the excerpts were to be published. Although he knew it was a bad idea, Robert blindly supported her. The press reacted with fury and Manchester spoke out. In the early hours of 16 January, the day the trial was due to begin, an agreement was reached. From that day and for a while, Bobby and Jackie's relationship seemed strained. He later confessed to a friend: "I just never wanted to spend the time on that."[36] Jackie may have resented Bobby for the agreement, as she cancelled their February holiday and they saw each other less for a while. A few days later, *Look* published the first episode of *The Death of a President*. It was an instant hit. The damage to Bobby and Jackie's popularity was great. Robert began to sink in the polls. A third of voters polled by Gallup said they thought less of Jackie, and 20 per cent of Bobby. In the autumn of 1966, according to a Harris poll, Robert led the incumbent President Johnson 53 per cent to 47 per cent. After the Manchester controversy, in March 1967, Johnson led 61 per cent to 39 per cent. Johnson, whom Bobby hated, exulted: "God, it just murders Bobby and Jackie both."[37]

The Manchester dispute took place while Robert's progressed Sun was quincunx Psyche, and on the day Jackie suited Manchester the orb of the aspect was of 0°01. The day the trial was to take place the orb was 0°04. On those days, when his love for Jackie blinded him to the point of jeopardising his reputation and career, the stakes of the Venus-Pluto opposition were particularly high. Psyche makes us question the way we've dealt with Venus, and Robert had to find a creative way to honour Venus in Capricorn on the midheaven opposite Pluto. The damaging aftermath of the Manchester controversy showed him that he'd given power to Jackie in the name of love. But Capricorn must stand by its views and risk loneliness to be true to itself. It's not a sign of compromise and accommodation, at least not when it comes to what it thinks is right, and not when it comes to its career. At the same time, Robert received unexpected help from his worst enemy, Lyndon Johnson, who forced him to take back his power and worship Venus again.

Although he hated him, Kennedy had muted his attacks on Johnson because they were both Democrats and he couldn't be seen to be betraying his fellow Democrats. However, the bombing in Vietnam was getting worse

---

36 Paul Brandus. *Jackie, her Transformation from First Lady to Jackie O.* (Post Hill Press 2020).
37 Evan Thomas, *Robert Kennedy: his life* (Simon & Schuster 2002).

and 33,000 Americans had already been killed. Bobby became very uncomfortable with his reticence. In December 1966 he began telling friends he was thinking about speaking out. But he was afraid of how Johnson might react: Kennedy believed that Johnson might increase the bombing simply because Robert had said the opposite. According to his biographer, Evan Thomas: "These were not entirely irrational fears. Johnson's hypersensitivity to Kennedy bordered on the pathological." Kennedy was so afraid of Johnson's irrationality that in his speeches he referred to him as "the Administration" to avoid mentioning his name. But again, this caution meant the power and decision-making was left in the hands of someone else. Jackie and Johnson, the beloved and the hated, prevented Robert from expressing himself.

During 1966, Kennedy had been through several transits implicating natal Uranus: the mid-life Uranus opposition to himself, and transits from Chiron and Saturn in Pisces. With Uranus in the twelfth house, there's no doubt the Promethean spirit within him, resonating with an oppressed collective, was awakening, so Kennedy wanted to speak out about the Vietnam War, to give peace a chance, but he felt trapped. Before he could make a decision, what he'd feared and tried to avoid at all costs happened: Johnson believed Kennedy had betrayed him. In early February 1967, Robert had just returned from a trip to Europe, where he'd tried to forget the Manchester controversy. In Paris he met a French Foreign Office official. Johnson sensed a plot, believing Kennedy was playing the diplomat and pressuring the President to negotiate with the North Vietnamese. Robert was summoned to the Oval Office where Johnson shouted at him and was very abusive, accusing him of having American blood on his hands. Shocking as it was, it was what Robert needed to feel free to speak out and was a turning point. On 2 March he gave his speech on the bombing, saying it was a horror and calling for a pause in the bombing. Johnson reacted: on 3 March, Kennedy was accused of masterminding the CIA plot to kill Fidel Castro. According to columnist Pearson, Castro decided to have JFK killed in revenge for this failed attempt. This was the worst blow: RFK's involvement in the plot was remote, but he'd always feared that his crusade against corruption and the mafia had something to do with his brother's assassination. The column just rubbed salt in his wounds.

His progressed Sun was 0°11 minutes past Psyche, but Robert was still at an impasse. After his speech, Johnson had stepped up the bombing and retaliated with Pearson's column. Pluto was still being projected onto others, and his Venus in Capricorn on the midheaven couldn't be fulfilled. One of his friends, Schlesinger, who saw Kennedy in April, felt his despair and wrote in his diary "an indefinable sense of depression hung over him as if he felt cornered by circumstance and did not know how to break out."

But an event eventually proved that Robert had learnt Psyche's lessons, albeit slowly and gradually, and was ready to embody power. After all, his birth chart had many placements suggesting a need to take responsibility, to have power and to be in the limelight: a stellium with the Sun in Scorpio and another with the Moon in Capricorn, his Venus-Pluto opposition on the IC/MC axis, his Jupiter right on the midheaven and his Moon in the tenth, making him sensitive to the needs of people. On 11 April 1967, Kennedy's duties as a member of a US Senate subcommittee on poverty took him to the Mississippi Delta to investigate the two-year-old War on Poverty programmes. He was deeply shocked by the scenes of want and deprivation, the stench and the vermin. He couldn't believe his eyes as he gazed at black children whose stomach were distended by starvation. Some were covered with sores. He returned to Washington and then flew to New York, where he told the wife of one of his aides: "You don't know what I saw! I have done nothing in my life! Everything I have done was a waste! Everything I have done was worthless!"[38] Robert's self-esteem was probably very low at that moment, but it was the day he decided to embrace his views, his struggles, his ambitions, and admit that people loved him and expected a lot from him. He resumed the cult of his Venus in Capricorn conjunct MC. He spent the following months looking for solutions, proposing innovative anti-poverty legislation using the tax code as a lever. He had to fight old senators and – again – Lyndon Johnson, who opposed the bill in the Senate. That summer, he began asking his relatives how they would react if he ran for president. They all encouraged him, except for Jackie. He was making up his mind and writing his destiny. He was being himself, standing by his values, fearing no one and nothing, not even Johnson, not even failure, not even Jackie's disapproval, not even death.

In RFK's chart, Psyche is in Gemini in the second house. This sign likes to make up its own mind, to learn for itself, to be informed: Robert's passage

---

38 Evan Thomas, *Robert Kennedy: his life* (Simon & Schuster 2002).

through the Delta enabled him to get information without an intermediary, and then to use Gemini's gift for language to speak up for those left behind. The second house represents his values well here, emphasised by the quincunx of the progressed Sun to Psyche. When he spoke out against the war in Vietnam, he was already revealing the qualities of his Psyche in Gemini. Until then, Robert had been more inclined to rely on the sign of Sagittarius to form his opinions: his Mercury is there, and Jupiter, his ruler, is particularly influential because he is exactly conjunct the midheaven. This sign can think according to acquired or transmitted beliefs, within a framework that can lack flexibility. Kennedy was strongly influenced by his Christian faith, but also by beliefs inherited from the Kennedy clan (in particular his father Joe). The qualities of Psyche in Gemini and her wisdom enabled Robert to take a more personal view at this crucial time in his life, to learn directly from the school of life and the field rather than from his family, his religion or his Greek philosophical readings. Of course, Sagittarius remained very important to him, and inspiring, but he needed a little of the wisdom of Gemini, just as Venus needed a little of the beauty of Proserpine.

RFK suffered greatly when his progressed Sun was quincunx his natal Psyche, but he also learned a lot. He couldn't let Jackie ruin his career, and neither could he let her decide who he should support. He didn't want to upset Johnson, but he had to speak his mind and stay true to his values. After mid-1967, having revealed the qualities of his Psyche, he was able to honour his Venus by taking a leadership position for Blacks and the poor, or pacifists, and fighting for what he valued. Most of his career had been spent in supporting roles, but he was ready to be a leader. His sense of his own worth was considerably triggered. Robert Kennedy, after Psyche, took back his power and didn't leave Pluto in the hands of others. He no longer had to choose between Pluto and Venus. By enacting his Scorpio Sun, he was willing to take risks, even the risk of being assassinated. Finally, as Liz Greene writes in her book *Relationships and How to Survive Them*, William Henley's poem Invictus is particularly suited to Scorpio: "I am the master of my fate, I am the captain of my soul."[39]

---

39 Liz Greene, *Relationships and How to Survive Them* (The Wessex Astrologer, 2023).

The Connection Between the Asteroid, the Myth and Projection

All these examples allow us to validate the link between the asteroid Psyche discovered in 1852 and the myth handed down by Apuleius 1,700 years before. The relational issues are particularly significant when the progressed Sun is within approximately 0°30 of orb of an aspect to Psyche (before and after the exact aspect). This covers a period of roughly one year. Prior to the exact aspect, the issues gradually fall into place, and often an event takes place shortly before or just after the exact aspect. In the case of Lennon, Robert Kennedy and Marie-Antoinette, for instance, the event took place the same week when their progressed Suns were in exact aspect to the natal asteroid, and in the case of Nerval, barely a week afterwards. The event can be the beginning of a love affair (Beauvoir), a break-up (Nerval, Nietzsche, Lennon, Montessori) or a confrontation (Madame du Châtelet, Marie-Antoinette, Robert Kennedy), sometimes even post-mortem, in the case of Proust.

In the examples we've seen, the suffering, the impasse in which they got stuck, or at the very least, a marked discomfort, led the people in question to experience Venus more authentically. It took Beauvoir six months to finally be able to write and proclaim "I am happy", Kennedy needed the same amount of time to start thinking about running for President, while fighting to make his bill to help the people of the Mississippi Delta pass the Senate. It also took Lennon about six months to be ready to take on his political and committed part, as can be seen in the *Imagine* album. Proust formed the idea of a book about his mother four months after the exact date, and *In Search of Lost Time* was probably still three or four months away. Six months was also the lapse of time it took one of my clients to decide to break off contact with her sister to protect her budding pregnancy, and another took the same length of time to decide to consult a centre specialising in violence against women. The data is consistent: several months are needed before a creative solution can be found and the cult of Venus can be restored.

Relationships are a means used by Psyche to make us unveil the qualities that are necessary for a healthy expression of Venus. These qualities can't be developed without the help of projection, which makes us see our own beauty in someone else, as Psyche who falls in love with Cupid's beauty, to finally possess it herself once she has become immortal. If the relationship causes us to suffer at the moment when our progressed Sun forms an aspect to Psyche, this is a way of enabling us to find within ourselves what we admired in the other person: we can thus take energy that was invested in the relationship, in a quest outside ourselves, and use it in a process that allows inner qualities to be revealed. The asteroid Psyche thus symbolises an immortal and divine inner beauty, because by giving Venus a chance to be honoured, these qualities (the virtues of the myth) will serve the Sun, and will contribute to giving a sense of life's uniqueness and meaning.

Of course, it's legitimate to wonder about the possibility of failure. What if you don't manage to honour Venus? Many criteria come into play: the position of Venus in the chart, her potentially difficult aspects, and above all her compatibility with the rest of the chart. A person who identifies more with Artemis or Ares might find it more difficult to pay homage to Venus. We also need to look at the transits of the period and other progressions, to understand the kairos and whether other issues could take over. Age, too, is an important parameter. However, whatever the solution found, each person in the study experienced their Venus more fully, once the Psyche episode was over. The feeling of self-esteem, but above all of being true to oneself, improved after several months. Yet the concept of happiness must be disconnected from that of self-esteem: for Nerval and Proust, there's a notion of a deliberate choice of suffering as a source of creation. For Marie Antoinette, being faithful to her Venus in Scorpio paradoxically meant temporary isolation, and as for Robert Kennedy, he then engaged in a struggle that was hardly conducive to happiness, but one that concomitantly triggered his sense of self-worth. As in the myth, it's the whole issue of the quest for self through the relationship that is underlined, and it goes beyond that of joy or happiness.

Part Three

The Astrological Psyche

In the previous chapter, the study of the effects of the aspects of the progressed Sun to the asteroid enabled us identify the themes involved when Psyche is triggered. This chapter will provide a general overview of the interpretation of the asteroid in astrology, based on her position in sign, her transits and her activation by the transits of the other planets. Finally, in the next chapter, natal aspects will be discussed, for they seem particularly significant and deserve to be addressed in more detail.

Psyche in the Birth Chart

Main points of the myth of Psyche

In order to understand the significance of the asteroid in the birth chart, a return to the core of the myth is necessary.

- at the beginning of the myth, a mortal beauty is worshipped instead of true beauty, the divine beauty represented by the goddess Venus
- Psyche must marry (enter into a relationship) because of this sin
- when she discovers the beauty of her divine husband (unveiling), she falls in love with him, loses him and sets off in search of him, driven by her love and the quest for true beauty
- the lunar goddesses refuse to help her
- Venus gives her the four labours, a series of tasks she must perform: the four labours allow Psyche to develop the four Platonic virtues
- when her labours are complete, Jupiter accepts the union of Psyche and Cupid. Psyche becomes immortal and marries Cupid
- Venus is satisfied because Jupiter told her the union is legitimate, between two gods
- Psyche gives birth to *Voluptas*

Elements of interpretation

Psyche, then, is a component of our chart that urges us to love and admire in another what belongs to us, but to which we can only gain access after certain stages of development, our "labours", have been completed. Apuleius compares the qualities Psyche must develop with the four Platonic virtues. Whatever we call them, these qualities need to be brought into a relationship if we're to create healthy, happy (Voluptas) and egalitarian emotional bonds that facilitate access to the self. In fact, the myth shows us they are necessary to satisfy Venus, to find our own worth, and then to become immortal, in other words to express our solar qualities. Immortality refers to the Sun, which gives meaning to our lives, makes them unique and connects them to the divine. As Dane Rudhyar puts it, when a person experiences a true metamorphosis, he becomes "more-than-man. He becomes one with the 'star' that is his spiritual essence."[40] Psyche's position in the chart helps us to clarify which virtues and qualities we need to develop, and for which we need the energy generated by a relationship and the issues it raises.

No interpretation of Psyche can be made without first looking at Venus's position in sign and house and her aspects, for Psyche gained immortality and divine beauty at the same time as Venus was again satisfied. Psyche's qualities may be more or less close to those valued by Venus, as, for example, with Newton who had Psyche in Libra and Venus in Aquarius, as opposed to when they are in square. But in any case, they are necessary for the full expression of the planet Venus, for the development of a sense of authenticity. The sign of Psyche tells us that the way we develop wisdom, moderation, courage and justice in our relationships will be according to the modalities of that sign. The archetype of wisdom may be Virgo, because of its discerning qualities, and the rulership and exaltation of Mercury, but each sign has its own wisdom that it's up to us to listen to. Capricorn, for example, can excel at discerning what deserves to be built up over time, what it can devote its efforts to, and what seems pointless. Moderation, which requires us to think before we act, might be easily accessible to air signs. Courage seems to be innate in signs ruled by Mars or in fire signs, but all signs have their own particular form of courage. Cancer has the courage to do what needs to be done to protect its inner self or others. Scorpio, which likes to venture into the realms of the unconscious, seems apt to develop the virtue of justice, but earth signs can maintain healthy boundaries, protecting themselves from the projections of others and giving them the right to protect themselves from its own.

---

40 Dane Rudhyar, *An Astrological Study of Psychological Complexes* (Shambhala 1976).

Finding oneself through relating

Relationships raising issues or producing suffering that allow us to reveal the qualities of our Psyche owe nothing to chance. When Psyche sees Cupid's divine beauty and falls in love with him, she is contemplating herself, for it's this beauty she will reveal thanks to her ultimate immortality. She must first succeed in her labours and drink the nectar, an alchemical symbol because it's the result of the transformation of the sap, the energy of which was used to produce the flower and then the nectar. Psyche must therefore undergo her metamorphosis in order to attain the beauty she loved in Cupid. In a similar way, we become attached to a person who possesses the same beauty as our Psyche, and then a feeling of dissatisfaction within the relationship leads us to appropriate this beauty, these qualities, once we've performed our own labours.

As mentioned above, the relationship between John Lennon and Paul McCartney had reached a point of no return when Lennon's progressed Sun shone on his natal Psyche. The latter is at 16°16 of Gemini and, importantly, exactly trine the Sun. In McCartney's chart, Mercury and the Sun are also in Gemini, at 18°21 and 26°39 respectively. There's also Uranus at 1°58 and Saturn at 5°13. Since the relationship between these two men was one of friendship, which they themselves described as fraternal, it's interesting to find McCartney's Mercury conjunct Lennon's Psyche. In his association with McCartney, Lennon had before his very eyes the embodiment of Gemini beauty, with this stellium consisting of the Sun and Mercury in the sign he rules. This beauty was irresistible to Lennon's Psyche, which, in trine to the Sun, was of great importance in the construction of his identity. Like Psyche, he fell in love with Gemini beauty in someone else. Then, at the time of the confrontation with the asteroid, he learned to make the beauty he admired his own. Venus watched over him and acted as a guide: it's Venus who set the work. In other words, it's this planet we must satisfy in order to find a form of immortal beauty within ourselves. Lennon went on to collaborate with a wide range of artists and political activists. He befriended the founders of the Youth International Party, a left-wing anti-war and anti-racist movement; supported pacifist movements and the Black Panthers; and collaborated with Frank Zappa, Mick Jagger, Harry Nilsson, Elton John and David Bowie, co-writing or producing songs. Here is the beauty of Gemini, with its adaptability, its love of freedom, its taste for eclectic encounters, its diverse interests, and its wise use of language.

Let's also look at the relationship between Nietzsche and Wagner. In the philosopher's chart, the asteroid is at 25°54 Capricorn, conjunct Saturn. In the same sign, in Wagner's chart, we find Saturn at 18°55. Since this relationship is of a son and a spiritual father, the presence of Saturn in cross-aspects is significant. Moreover, Nietzsche's Psyche is conjunct Saturn in his natal chart, so he wasn't only seeking the beauty of Capricorn, but also of Saturn within himself. He was therefore captivated by the beauty of his surrogate father's Saturn in Capricorn. After the encounter between his progressed Sun and Psyche, he was able to incarnate Saturn and his wisdom. As he so aptly put it: "I now live my aspiration to wisdom, down to the smallest detail, whereas earlier I only revered and idolized the wise."[41]

In Simone de Beauvoir's chart, Psyche is at 10°07 Scorpio. In Sartre's chart, Mars is at 8°27 Scorpion, in conjunction to Beauvoir's Psyche. In order to find the beauty of Scorpio within herself, Beauvoir was attracted to her lover's Mars: in the context of a romantic relationship, this is not surprising. In the same way, John Fitzgerald Kennedy, for example, who had Psyche in Virgo and for whom the encounter between the progressed Sun and Psyche led to the separation from his great love, Inga Arvard, was attracted by the beauty of his lover's Venus in Virgo.

The other attracts us, subjugates us, but what it's all about lies within: when Psyche contemplates Cupid's beauty, she doesn't yet know that she'll become just as beautiful, having been granted immortality. Madame du Châtelet had Psyche at 28°13 Leo. In the chart of Koenig, the mathematician who did her so much harm, there is a stellium in Leo composed of Mercury, the Sun, Venus and Saturn. It's easy to see why she expected so much from him, even though he only served to show her that the beauty of Leo was within her. It's no coincidence that Marie-Antoinette, whose Psyche is at 26°20 Taurus, had a very close relationship with her mother, the Empress of Austria: the latter has a stellium in Taurus made up of Mercury, the Sun, Neptune and Venus. Above all, her mother's Mercury is at 26°20 Taurus, in perfect conjunction to her daughter's Psyche. There's

---

41 Friedrich Nietzsche, *Selected Letters of Friedrich Nietzsche*, ed. and trans. Christopher Middleton (University of Chicago Press, 1969).

no doubt that Marie-Antoinette must have admired her mother's intelligence, insight and power. But at the end of her struggle with the latter, due to Madame du Barry, Marie-Antoinette was able to develop the virtues of Taurus within herself. In particular, we know she fled the intrigues of the court to her little Trianon, where she enjoyed her own farm and theatre and tried to live as simply as possible. Above all, for the rest of her life, and in particular during the French Revolution, she demonstrated the qualities of determination and tenacity so dear to Taurus.

Gérard de Nerval had a close conjunction between Psyche and Uranus, at 0°09 and 1°50 Scorpio respectively. In the chart of Jenny Colon, with whom he fell in love, Uranus is at 5°50 Scorpio and the Sun is at 12°48 of the same sign. Nerval was therefore fascinated by the beauty of Uranus in Scorpio, which was his own, but which he could only possess through the other, since the planet was conjunct Psyche in his natal chart. With this Sun-Uranus conjunction, Colon naturally radiated the qualities of Scorpio and allowed Nerval to make them his own. Venus reigns over the arts: satisfying her by developing the virtues of Uranus in Scorpio (as he conjoins natal Psyche) could only nourish the poet's creativity. His Uranian creativity would be constantly stimulated by his lost relationship, and he would be able to plunge into the depths of Scorpio to give his work its potential to penetrate the human soul.

Psyche by house

The house in which Psyche is placed gives an idea of the realm, the field of experience, in which the qualities represented by the asteroid are most easily expressed and then put at the service of Venus and the sense of self-worth. For example, Robert Kennedy, John Lennon and Friedrich Nietzsche had Psyche in the second house, and they focused on their personal values after the activation of Psyche by the progressed Sun. Simone de Beauvoir had Psyche in the eleventh house, and her relationship with Sartre allowed her to become involved in associations and groups with a universal vocation, such as existentialists and feminists, and to found the magazine *Les Temps modernes* with other intellectuals. When a planet in progression or in transit makes an important aspect to our natal Psyche, the house in which she's placed can also give information about the kind of "labour" that will be required of us and the field of experience that will be affected.

Psyche by sign

Here are a few points to ponder about the qualities that need to be expressed according to the sign in which Psyche is placed in the birth chart. Of course, it's important to remember that no sign can be briefly described, so these are only suggestions. In addition, the house in which Psyche is located, and especially her aspects to other planets of the chart, greatly influence her qualities and her role in the person's life. These qualities need to be put at the service of Venus and the Sun. Developed through a relationship, they're meant not only to enable us to flourish in emotional relationships but also to increase our sense of personal worth.

Psyche in Aries

We're attracted to the qualities of Aries and seek to develop them in ourselves through a relationship. These can include a capacity for initiative, a willingness to take risks, to seek out new experiences and to be a force of suggestion. The wisdom of Aries should enable us to recognise when we need to leave a stable and peaceful position in order to move forward, and when we should instead reflect, step back and exercise moderation. Aries is ruled by Mars and is where the Sun is exalted. The qualities of these two planets are therefore important and indicate the extent to which assertiveness, the ability to assert oneself and defend one's rights, needs to be developed in emotional relationships. Within a relationship, the feeling of being able to change the course of our lives at any time, if we so wish, through our will and actions, is essential to our fulfilment. Any restriction or feeling we can't carry out new projects because of the bonds we've established will be detrimental to our personal expression and to the joy Venus could bring.

Psyche in Taurus

The qualities of Taurus are secretly buried within us, and we need to admire them in someone else to make them our own. Venus rules this sign, so Psyche in Taurus may seem a natural way to serve the goddess. Taurus's taste for beauty is likely to be a very important lever in our inner quest, and trying to define what we find beautiful and what we value will be crucial. The Moon is exalted in Taurus, so it's important to know how to take our inner self, our emotions and our needs into account when we get involved in an emotional relationship. Then the tenacity and practical abilities of the sign will certainly be important qualities in staying anchored to our values.

Psyche in Gemini

Like John Lennon, who found in Paul McCartney an excellent projective support for his Psyche in Gemini, our wisdom may be related to the great adaptability of the sign, its love of freedom, its eclecticism and its ability to learn from its experiences – like Maria Montessori – rather than from pre-established dogmas. The use of written or spoken language seems to be very important in daring to confront the emotional realm, a confrontation necessary for the establishment of Venusian relationships that respect justice, in the Platonic sense of the term. In the case of Psyche, the qualities of Gemini are less likely to be used to turn away from feelings or to try to understand everything rather than to feel: they are at the service of creating a bond in which emotional involvement is clarified by putting it into words. The idea of individual freedom within the couple is also important.

Psyche in Cancer

The lunar goddesses refuse to help Psyche, but Psyche in Cancer needs to question the Moon and the conditioning of early childhood in order to form meaningful and happy Venusian partnerships. Psyche in Cancer is an invitation to listen to the inner child, to return to the past and to oneself, before forming relationships which might otherwise be no more than a repetition of those experienced with one's parents. The Venusian function can be hindered if the Moon hasn't served as a mirror for the light of the child's Sun during their development, and it's the wisdom of Psyche in Cancer to understand this and to take care of one's inner self before being able to share it authentically with another person. Similarly, the exaltation of Jupiter in this sign indicates that what has been taken care of can then expand and develop, and encourages people with Psyche in Cancer to have the courage and wisdom to choose emotional relationships in which they can grow and develop.

Psyche in Leo

The person who has attracted our attention is likely to have an innate gift for taking centre stage and shining, or great self-confidence, like Koenig, who so impressed Madame du Châtelet. Leo's wisdom lies in knowing that one's own brilliance shouldn't be hindered by an emotional relationship, but should find its place within it. Venus, "golden" and "smiling" according to Hesiod, is indeed at the service of the Sun, and her mirror shows us that relationships help us to know ourselves, to get closer to ourselves. Psyche in Leo is therefore an invitation to take the risk of expressing ourselves through relationships, to be an individual in the truest sense of the word, even within a couple, and to know how to choose what we want to communicate to the world about ourselves, how we want to radiate.

Psyche in Virgo

This position is illustrated by Psyche's first labour, the sorting of seeds. Mercury rules this sign, but it's also the sign of his exaltation. Our qualities of discrimination, associated with our intellectual abilities, will of course be at the forefront of our worship of Venus. We need to develop within ourselves the ability to sort out what belongs to us and what doesn't, to maintain a healthy immunity to our environment and our emotional relationships, to ensure Venus's need for harmony and concord never forces us to be "for sale" by pleasing others without respecting our own choices.

Psyche in Libra

The person we're attracted to may be socially comfortable or have a gift for creating harmony in the physical world or in relationships. Venus rules Libra, as she does Taurus, but here, rather than emphasising values, this position emphasises justice, in the sense of Saturn's exaltation in this sign. Our inner beauty, once revealed, enables us to create fair partnerships in which everyone's status as a subject is respected, as are differences of opinion. The ideal relationship is one in which each partner recognises the right of the other to play their own role, to step outside the expectations or projections of the other, and to be different from the representations they may have had of the ideal partner.

Psyche in Scorpio

People who seem to easily understand the hidden reasons why people behave irrationally, or who are at ease with the world of emotions or the unconscious, can attract us at a time when our inner beauty is ready to be revealed. Uranus is exalted in Scorpio, which means we can combine Plutonian depth with Uranian vision and his ability to break the chains of our enslavement. Psyche in Scorpio invites us to introspection, to inner transformation, to try to understand what's going on in the shadows. A confrontation with our buried emotions and our relationship with power, within the couple, is necessary to satisfy Venus fully and authentically.

Psyche in Sagittarius

Sagittarius is evoked in the third work, and its courage is highlighted, as well as its ability to dive in after seeing things from above. Psyche in this sign invites us to define our own vision of things and the meaning we give to love or friendship. We have the feeling that life has meaning, that chance doesn't exist and covers another reality of which emotional relationships are one manifestation. The choice of partner or friend must therefore be made with this vision and inspiration in mind. Psyche's first task, sorting the seeds, comes to mind: Psyche in Sagittarius must know how to choose what's compatible with her vision and, above all, what gives meaning to her life.

Psyche in Capricorn

Nietzsche exemplifies Psyche in the sign of Capricorn, ruled by Saturn. Saturn and Venus seem at first sight to be reluctant to spend time together, and natal Venus-Saturn aspects have a reputation for being difficult to live with. However, the birth of Aphrodite owes everything to Cronus-Saturn, as she was born from the castration of Ouranos by the latter. What's more, Saturn is exalted in Libra. Psyche in this sign is therefore an invitation to take into account the Saturnian law in the couple, the law that sees in it the union of two autonomous and independent beings who love each other, not to serve as substitute parents or providers of emotional or material security. Saturn favours the meeting of two beings who don't need each other, but who enjoy being together and find meaning in it, an opportunity for growth. Finally, Mars is exalted in Capricorn, which means Psyche in

Capricorn can come close to Psyche in Aries in the need to develop assertiveness in relationships. Psyche in Capricorn therefore asks us to develop our inner strength and capacity for solitude and to take full responsibility for ourselves without needing anyone else's approval or help.

Psyche in Aquarius

The wisdom of Aquarius, as we shall see in the next chapter with Jacqueline Kennedy, is to know, like Capricorn, how to maintain independence in the relationship, but also how to maintain a certain fruitful distance, a space in which the individual can grow and express himself. It's ruled by both Saturn and Uranus. Aquarius thus evokes justice in the Platonic sense of the word, because it knows how to protect itself from the projections of others, thanks to the space it maintains between itself and the other person, which allows it to establish healthy boundaries. Of course, Psyche in Aquarius also asks us to add to the desires of our Venus based on the sign she's in, the need for intellectual or fraternal companionship. Each time Psyche is activated, we're invited to reconsider our ideals, to remain faithful to them and to ensure the relationship supports them.

Psyche in Pisces

Psyche in this sign demands that the plunge into the world of emotion described in the third work be made with the aim of connecting with something greater, luminous, numinous. Whichever sign Venus is in, relationships have to respect the need to feel in deep communion with the other, to share something that goes beyond the mundane and the visible. Venus is exalted in Pisces: the wisdom of this sign lies in its vision of love, of which we should ask ourselves each time Psyche is activated whether we have remained faithful. This vision can go as far as that of Lucius (the one who was turned into a donkey) and Plato, i.e. a connection to the divine through love, or simply the love of the divine, for example, the primordial goddess, Isis for Lucius. With Psyche in Pisces, we can go in search of a union that gives us the impression of entering another dimension, one in which love gives us access to the divine within us, to our divine part.

When Psyche Causes Suffering

To be fully experienced, the qualities of the sign of Psyche need the mediation of another person. When we admire someone, especially when the relationship causes suffering, it can be useful to look at which planets in that person's chart our Psyche echoes. We should use the example before us to discover something authentic and beautiful inside ourselves that hasn't yet been developed. The house in which the asteroid is placed gives us further clues as to the area of experience in which these qualities can be fully developed. For example, if Psyche is in the second house, her sign will express itself preferentially in terms of values. If Psyche is in the third house, her qualities may be expressed in the use of language.

All suffering must be understood as a necessary but unbearable longing that enables us to embark on an inner quest. Psyche suffers from the lack of Cupid, otherwise she wouldn't carry out her labours. Venus is the guide, the one who decides what trials must be overcome, because she's the guardian of true beauty, eternal and divine beauty. So, when we find ourselves suffering in a relationship, it's always fruitful to examine how we have honoured Venus in the past. Have we been true to ourselves, or have we worshipped substitutes? Do we know what our values are and are we able to respect them in our choices, including love? Have we found the gold within us that creates feelings of self-love and self-esteem? Any activation of Psyche is an opportunity to further develop the qualities she symbolises and to draw closer to Venus. This is especially true when the progressed Sun comes into resonance with the asteroid: in some cases, this can be a real earthquake in our lives. The transits of Psyche, on the other hand, are like little repetitions, key moments that allow us to move forward in an ever more accomplished but never really finished quest.

Psyche in Transit

Between Mars and Jupiter

Psyche takes about five years to complete one revolution around the Sun, but she stays in each sign for very different lengths of time, from about two months to more than ten months when she turns retrograde. For example, Psyche was in Scorpio from 1 November 2022 to 4 October 2023, or 10½ months, while she was only in Sagittarius from 4 October to 26 December, or 2½ months. This was due to a long retrograde in Scorpio. Thus, she passed over certain degrees of Scorpio three times and only once over each degree of Sagittarius, suggesting that her effects will be felt more gradually in certain signs, with a retrograde phase that may be a phase of awareness. Psyche in transit has a duration of influence somewhere between that of Mars and Jupiter, depending on whether she's retrograde or not. On average, she's 2.65 times slower than Mars and 2.38 times faster than Jupiter.

Apart from her periods of retrograde motion, her passage through each degree of the zodiac is fairly brief, staying for about two days. Unless we keep a diary, we probably won't remember what happened during a Psyche transit. The same goes for the client in the consultation, who may not remember anything, as is often the case with transits of fast-moving planets. But if you go back over your notes from day to day, it's possible to see what issues a Psyche transit might have raised. The effects are easiest to see when she turns retrograde and passes over the same point three times, staying in the same sign for more than six months. This longer period seems to offer the opportunity for a more substantial transformation. It is, of course, a relationship that sets this in motion: as we have already seen, it could be a meeting, a separation, a disappointment, a confrontation, or growing unease about the behaviour of a third party that suddenly seems intolerable. The person can be a spouse, child, relative, friend or colleague. It could also be a therapist, for the work of a psychotherapist, psychoanalyst or astrologer is to help the client, through the relationship that develops, to understand and know themself and to bring out what's been kept unconscious.

Psyche aspecting natal planets or points

When Psyche in transit aspects one of our natal planets, a relationship invites us to question the way in which we've lived this planet up to that point, always with the aim of achieving greater authenticity. Let's take the example of transiting Psyche in conjunction to natal Chiron: the mythological figure of the centaur is of a healer, a doctor, an orphan, an adoptive father and a teacher, who has been unfairly wounded and whose wound is incurable. At the moment of a conjunction to the transiting asteroid, a relationship can hit where it hurts. Something wounded or inadequate in us may resurface, the nature of which will depend on the position of Chiron in the birth chart: if Chiron is in the eighth house, we may feel sexually insecure; if Chiron is in the first house, we may feel inadequate, in a position of inferiority; if Chiron is in the third house, we may find it difficult to communicate in the relationship or feel unheard. But once again, the relationship must be seen as a means and not an end: if this wound is felt, it's because it's always been there in the unconscious, doing invisible undermining work that's harmful to our self-esteem. The relationship exposes a painful feeling, but allows it to be brought into consciousness. It's an invitation to take on Chiron's other role, that of healer, for ourselves.

A separation or estrangement can reawaken a poorly integrated natal Uranus: for example, Psyche in transit opposed John Lennon's natal Uranus when he began his eighteen-month separation from Yoko Ono and began living with another woman. One of my acquaintances, after taking a course in self-discovery through theatre, felt the spark she needed to leave a job that had become too limiting and follow the path she'd always enjoyed. During the course she met a coach who convinced her of her talent, and this happened when Psyche was conjunct her Uranus. The encounter was brief, but the effects were long-lasting.

Finally, it's also interesting to note the days when Psyche is in transit over the North or South Node: during this period, which can last up to 4–5 days, a relationship, often new (but not necessarily) can make us rethink our life path or confirm it, questioning the way we have lived the values of the transited sign. The relationship may be very brief: it may be a single encounter, but it can be crucial in bringing about a new awareness. I had no idea at the time, but on the day of my very first consultation as an astrologer, Psyche in transit was exactly conjunct my South Node. I didn't see much of my first client after that, but her feedback completely confirmed my decision to go down this path. This fleeting relationship, which lasted a little over an hour, was nonetheless decisive.

As with any transit, it's useful to look at the asteroid's natal position, including the house she's in and her aspects, to refine the analysis and understand what experiences and emotions the relationship is helping us to grow through.

Psyche, a catalyst for slower transits

Psyche transits often act as a trigger, intensifying the transit of an outer planet. Let's take the example of a transit of Saturn over Venus: its effects can be felt for a year. When Psyche joins Saturn, it's an important moment in the planet's transit. Just as Mars tends to bring the outward manifestation of an outer planet transit, Psyche seems to mean that problems in a relationship will serve to manifest the transit of another planet. Similarly, if transiting Pluto is squaring the Moon, his effects could be felt for at least two to three years. Nevertheless, if Psyche in transit conjoins the Moon, or if the progressed Moon conjoins Psyche, these moments will be very significant. A relationship will then be the means chosen by Pluto to exert his effects on the Moon. Another way of putting it is that the effects of Psyche are amplified by Pluto, which has opened a deep and powerful channel of energy that the asteroid can use to help us grow through a relationship, whether the moment is pleasant or not.

One of my clients, aged 44, had been going through a transit of Chiron in square to Venus for about eight months. She told me that many issues of discord with her husband had come up during this time, without her really knowing why she was so angry with him. Then came Christmas, when she saw her mother. During the festive season, her mother behaved in such a shocking way towards another member of the family that my client suddenly realised there was no excuse she could find for her. It was then she realised there was something wrong with her mother, and the way she'd treated her as a child was ultimately unacceptable. And she put her finger on her Venusian problem: a deep and abiding, but unspoken, feeling that she didn't deserve love because her mother didn't seem to show her any. On the day of her mother's shocking behaviour with this other person, Psyche was exactly conjunct her natal Venus. The underlying reflection was related to Chiron and the childhood wound (the client also had a natal Venus-Chiron opposition), but Psyche provided the trigger for her awareness.

1969: Paul McCartney's terrible year

To study the effects of Psyche transits, it's necessary to date events to the day, which is difficult to do unless the people involved have been taking daily notes. But The Beatles were observed, even spied on, every single day of their career, so we have enough evidence to illustrate the effects of Psyche in transit on Paul McCartney's life in 1969.

The year began with the recording of the *Let it Be* album, for which McCartney had the idea of filming their rehearsals, with a view to making a TV or film programme and turning their work into a concert, as in the good old days. But the atmosphere was tense from the start – Yoko Ono's constant presence at Lennon's side was largely to blame. But the death of their manager Brian Epstein a few months earlier and McCartney's desperate attempt to take control of the band to prevent its demise also contributed. The cameras didn't help either. McCartney's attitude became increasingly rigid and controlling, and Harrison criticised him for telling him what to do. On 6 January, he was recorded telling McCartney: "I'll play what you want me to play. Or I won't play at all if you don't want me to. Whatever it is that'll please you, I'll do it." On 10 January, exhausted after a morning spent arguing with McCartney, Harrison decided to leave the band. He finally returned on 15 January. At the time this series of incidents began, Psyche had just conjoined McCartney's IC. The Beatles were truly his home, his roots, at this time, and Psyche's opposition to the midheaven shows the impact of the relationship problems with Harrison on McCartney's career. Meanwhile, Lennon was being transformed by the drugs he was taking with Yoko, and one can only imagine the effect on the strong-willed, perfectionist McCartney as he tried to save the sinking ship. According to Lennon: "I would just tag along and I had Yoko by then. I didn't even give a s**t about anything. I was stoned all the time, too, on H etc."⁴² On his return on 15 January, Harrison put himself in a position to demand what he wanted in exchange for his return: he had the recording location changed and cancelled McCartney's concert plans. The negotiations lasted five hours, during which Harrison made it clear he would have no problem leaving The Beatles if he didn't get what he wanted.

A little later, McCartney quarrelled with Lennon to the point of not inviting him to his wedding to Linda Eastman, which took place on 12 March when she was pregnant. They went on honeymoon on 16 March. It may seem surprising that at the same time transiting Mars in Sagittarius was opposing McCartney's natal Psyche at 8°18 Virgo. But in fact, on the eve of their wedding, he'd had a huge argument with his future wife and almost called the whole thing off. He'd also just had a row with Lennon. When Lennon heard about the wedding, he declared McCartney was dead to him and decided to get married himself on 14 March. He left for France to get married on the same day that Paul left for his honeymoon in the USA. McCartney's natal Psyche was therefore affected by the opposition of Mars, which certainly forced him to rely on the innate discernment and moderation of Virgo in order not to cancel his wedding or have his honeymoon ruined by Lennon's reactions.

In April, Psyche entered Aquarius, a sign in which she spent many months as she turned retrograde. For McCartney, early Aquarius is an important position, as he has a Mars-Pluto conjunction in early Leo in his birth chart. This conjunction is probably at the root of his need for control, but also his temper tantrums, which were well hidden but have been reported by various sources, and his jealousy. It's also surely one of the sources of his inexhaustible creativity and insatiable energy, as it's in Leo. At the time of Psyche's first opposition to the Mars-Pluto conjunction, McCartney decided on his own that the version of the single "Get Back" being played on the BBC was unsatisfactory. Just as the single was about to be released, he returned to the studio alone to remix it. The attitude of control, of taking power over the band, is palpable. This was also the moment when he and Lennon reconciled after their falling-out the previous month, and the two of them recorded "The Ballad of John and

---

42 Jann S. Wenner. *Lennon remembers: The Full Rolling Stone Interviews from 1970* (New York: Verso, 2000).

Yoko", a song about Lennon's wedding and honeymoon, just as Psyche was coming to terms with McCartney's Mars-Pluto conjunction. You can sense that the issue of power and control in the band was at stake, with McCartney vacillating between taking a unilateral decision on "Get Back" and bowing to Lennon's wish to evoke his relationship with Yoko (and put her photo on the album cover) in a Beatles song.

When Psyche left this position in May, she moved into opposition to Paul's natal Chiron at 12°09 Leo. On 8 May 1969, Lennon signed a contract on behalf of The Beatles, formally appointing Allen Klein as their manager. (The problems posed by this man have already been discussed in Part Two, in the section on Lennon.) On 9 May, the other three Beatles demanded that McCartney also sign, but he refused. In the evening, Psyche was at 11°30 Leo opposite Paul's natal Chiron. A violent argument broke out and McCartney found himself alone in the studio at 11 p.m. He was fortunate that Steve Miller arrived to record that evening and, seeing McCartney alone and miserable, listened to him, then they recorded a track together: "My Dark Hour", for which McCartney was credited under a pseudonym. This Chiron in Leo and in the eleventh house conjoins the Moon and suggests McCartney may feel excluded from groups and associations in general, or socially inadequate and emotionally isolated. Being truly himself and shining (Leo) may be felt as a threat of rejection or isolation. The other three Beatles joining forces and sidelining him certainly reopened this wound, but the presence of Steve Miller reminds us of the two sides of Chiron, the wounded healer, for this session showed Paul how much his talent as a musical creator could bring him comfort, a form of healing. In both cases, relationships (Psyche) had awakened Chiron. McCartney later commented: "It was a very strange time in my life and I swear I got my first grey hairs that month."[43]

The return of Psyche by retrograde, in opposition to the Mars-Pluto conjunction, came at the moment of the birth of McCartney's first child: Mary, on 28 August 1969, when Psyche had returned to 3°45 Aquarius. At a time when The Beatles' existence was hanging by a thread, when he was doing everything he could to save them, he had to deal with a major change in his personal life and accept he was losing control of it, at least

---

43 The Beatles, *The Beatles Anthology* (Chronicle Books, 2000).

for a while, as anyone who has welcomed a newborn child into their home knows.

Psyche resumed her forward march, and she again opposed the natal Mars-Pluto conjunction: on 20 September, when Psyche was exactly opposite Mars, Lennon announced he was leaving the band. McCartney managed to keep it a secret for a while, but he knew he'd lost everything he'd fought for over the last year, and everything he'd built up over the last ten years. Mars-Pluto's need for control was being undermined by a relationship, and the anger it could hold probably overwhelmed McCartney.

Throughout the year, Chiron moved in and out of early Aries, in trine to this natal Mars-Pluto conjunction. This major, long transit invited McCartney to rethink his need for control and how he should direct his creative energy. But the moments when Psyche was opposite the natal conjunction were the moments when his relationships (Lennon, the other Beatles, Linda, and his daughter Mary) acted as triggers to question these issues.

Transits and progressions to Psyche

Planets in transit aspecting Psyche, especially in conjunction, activate the themes associated with the asteroid: the need to develop the qualities of the sign of Psyche, especially within a relationship. It's also about questioning our loyalty to Venus, and therefore our values and self-esteem. With the myth in mind, we need to see how faithful we are to who we are (justice), whether we know what we value and whether we can make our choices accordingly (wisdom), and whether we have the courage to assert these choices and the moderation to act after reflection.

How Psyche is activated depends on which planet is visiting her. The progressed Sun is particularly interesting because it enlightens, i.e., enables consciousness, and its passage over Psyche is a stage in the process of individuation. (Its effects have been discussed at length in Part Two.) The type of inner or outer experience triggered by Psyche depends on the nature of the transiting or progressed planet, and the usual rules of astrological interpretation apply. We might add that sometimes the planet also seems to indicate the nature of the relationship involved: if it's the Moon, it's not uncommon for it to be a parent-child relationship; if it's Saturn or Jupiter, it may be a mentor; if it's Venus, it will be of a romantic nature. But these rules are far from rigid, because a relationship of a loving nature can very well be the source of a Jupiterian experience, for instance.

The return of Psyche is also a moment to watch out for: it's as if every five years we have to reflect on what we value and how we may have violated one of these values in one of our relationships. It's likely an external event, such as the behaviour of the person with whom we have this relationship, will be the cause of this new questioning, the scale and scope of which won't reach the possible earthquakes accompanying the arrival of the progressed Sun under the influence of the asteroid. Nevertheless, these occasions can be fruitful if we're prepared to do the necessary work: generally causing less suffering, they can be forgotten as soon as they pass, but they can also give rise to conscious work aimed at questioning our values.

Part Four

Psyche in Aspect

Psyche in Aspect to the Sun

To try to understand the effects of an aspect between the asteroid and the Sun in the birth chart, it's worth looking at charts where the aspect is as close as possible: Richard Wagner is an excellent example with his exact quincunx between Psyche and the Sun.

Richard Wagner

Richard was born in Leipzig in 1813, at the height of the Napoleonic Wars. He was the ninth child of Friedrich Wagner, a police officer, and Johanna, née Petz. Because of the fighting in the region, hospitals were full, there was no time to bury the corpses, and horses rotted in the Elster. The situation was ripe for epidemics, and Richard's father contracted typhus and died on 23 November, when his son was six months old. In her misfortune, Richard's mother could count on a family friend, Ludwig Geyer, who married her in August 1814 and claimed her seven surviving children as his own. Richard grew up thinking of his stepfather as his own father, later referring to him as "our father Geyer"; but in 1821, when he was eight years old, he had to face the loss of this surrogate father. Wagner thus lost his father for the second time: this time the man who had played this role. The death of a father during childhood is always of particular significance and undoubtedly influences the behaviour of those who must deal with it. For Wagner, the theme of the father was truly at the heart of his work and remained so until his last days. In addition to the loss, he'd to grow up with unanswered questions: his father had left nothing personal, not even a portrait, so he never knew what he looked like. Wagner's last wife, Cosima, thought his real father might have been Geyer, which Wagner refused to believe, but no one knew what he really thought. On his deathbed, he made sure to tell his son Siegfried everything about himself in order to spare him the pain that would haunt him for the rest of his life. He also systematically wrote down every detail of his life, "Mein Leben", to pass on to his son.

Paternal issues, and more broadly issues of identity, are at the heart of many of Wagner's works. The Sun in square to Chiron seems to reflect these solar doubts, but the exact quincunx between the Sun and Psyche provides additional information. The aspect can be read in both directions: in order to establish his individual identity, Wagner had to develop the qualities of Psyche. But these qualities are first seen in the father, an archetypal solar figure who should have served as Cupid at the beginning of his life. We can therefore imagine a constant tug-of-war between the need to develop Psyche in Scorpio and the lack of a relationship that would have generated sufficient admiration and desire to reveal Psyche. Problems related to the death of the father or ignorance of his identity recur in the lives of Wagner's heroes. He began composing as a teenager, and between the ages of fourteen and fifteen he worked on *Leubald*, a tragedy that was never completed and which he believed to be lost. In this early work, the father of the hero was murdered. *Leubald* promises his father's ghost that he'll kill all the members of his murderer's family, then commits a series of murders and descends into madness. In his *Tetralogy* there's a succession of heroes, Siegmund and Siegfried, both with prominent father issues. In *The Valkyrie*, Siegmund is the son of Wotan, who never revealed to him who he was during the time he spent with him on Earth. Siegmund calls his father Wolfe and doesn't know the truth about his personal history. His son Siegried, who appears in the drama of the same name, was born after his father's death. He's unaware that the man raising him is his adoptive father, who tells him so at the beginning of the opera, at the same time as revealing his origins. In *Tristan and Isolde*, as in the legend, Tristan lost his father before he was born. Walther von Stolzing in *The Mastersingers of Nuremberg* has lost his father and his mother. Finally, Parsifal in the first act of the eponymous tragedy has even forgotten his own name and has no idea his parents are dead.

Venus has a unique place and importance in Wagner's chart: she's the ruler of the chart, conjunct the ascendant and the Sun, and trine the midheaven, and she's in the sign she rules, Taurus, where Mercury, ruler of the Sun, is also placed. We've seen the close relationship between Venus and Psyche, and here they are in close quincunx (less than 1° orb). Wagner's quest for identity was also a Venusian quest, and he was naturally drawn to art, as Venus is in Taurus. The connections between Psyche, the Sun and Venus suggest Wagner needed to establish a meaningful relationship

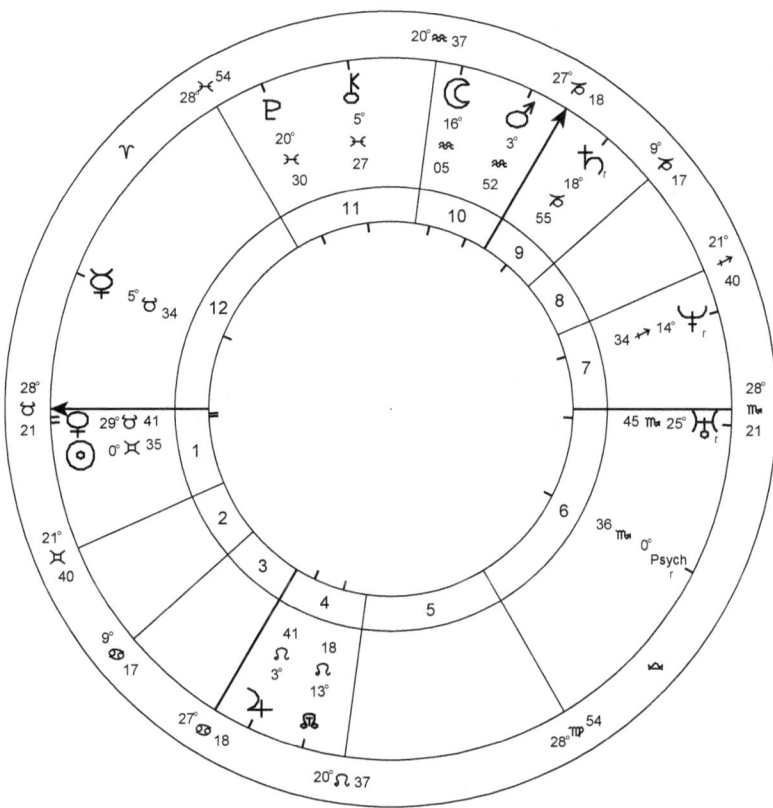

(Psyche) with his father in order to define his identity (Sun) and give himself value (Venus). Returning again and again to the theme of the fatherless hero, Wagner, haunted by his confusion about his origins, sought to shed light on the question of parentage throughout his life, just as Psyche sought to find out who her husband was. In this respect, it's particularly interesting to note that the forbidden revelation appears in two of his works.

In *The Fairies*, the first opera Wagner completed but that was never performed in his lifetime, the hero Arindal learns, as we have come to expect from Wagner, that his father has died. He then explains he has married a fairy, Ada, on condition that he promises *not to find out who she is* for eight years. He's unable to keep his promise and is banished from the fairy kingdom. Ada must become mortal to find her husband, but complications result in her being turned to stone, and it's Arindal who breaks the spell with the help of a lyre. Through his courage and love, he achieves immortality and reigns over the fairy kingdom with Ada. Final immortality is another common thread with the myth of Psyche. In *Lohengrin*, a mature work (1850), a young princess, Elsa, is accused of murdering her brother. A mysterious knight appears and offers to face God's judgement by fighting for the princess's honour, and then to marry her – on one condition: *that she doesn't try to find out where he comes from or who he is*. The knight quickly defeats her accuser, Telramund, spares his life and marries Elsa. But the defeated and humiliated knight broods over his revenge with his wife: the two of them, like Psyche's two sisters, sow doubt in the princess's mind about the origins of the mysterious knight – until she asks the forbidden question. The knight then reveals his divine nature and the meaning of his sacred mission, and disappears forever.

Unable to rely on his relationship with his father to reveal Psyche, Wagner managed to live with this early amputation in a creative way: intuitively sensing that beauty laid in what remained unknown to him, he set the stage for heroes and heroines who didn't know their origins or the identity of the person with whom they fell in love. His father was thus the archetypal figure of mystery on which Wagner based most of his work. The question of origin is omnipresent in Wagner's work, as are those of identity and loss. Love and relationships are marked by the blurring of the protagonists' identities; what is hidden is essential, as in the myth of Psyche. In *Lohengrin*, the "pure and brave" knight whose identity Elsa was forbidden to ask, and who disappeared as soon as she asked the forbidden question, gives her back the twin brother she lost when she was a teenager, before leaving for his kingdom forever. In *Tristan and Isolde*, Isolde is also unaware of Tristan's identity, which turns out to be that of her lover's murderer. Unwilling to live by betraying her first love, but madly in love with Tristan, she chooses to unite with him in death and dies of love over her lover's body. In *The Valkyrie*, Siegmund finds refuge in an unknown house, where the unknown woman who takes him in turns out to be his twin sister, lost years before and never recognised – they fall in love. In *Twilight of the Gods*, Siegfried falls victim to a potion that makes him forget his beloved Brünnhilde. It's only when she dies that he relives his love for her and truly understands who she is. Brünnhilde chooses to join him in death by burning herself at the stake.

Psyche begins her quest and her labours after she's seen Cupid and has revealed his beauty. Wagner, on the other hand, seems to have remained stuck, oil lamp in hand, trying in vain to illuminate his Cupid, the one he'd missed all his life. So he tried to portray heroes who shared the same loss and the same questions as himself, searching through his work for what would enable him to reconnect with the lost divine. His relationship with Cosima may have seemed stable and happy, but on closer inspection, at the time his progressed Sun in Leo was squaring Psyche, Wagner was in the throes of a passionate love affair with Theodore's daughter Judith Gautier. Cosima made several references in her diary to his preoccupied state and bad temper, which she blamed on money problems. This was Wagner's last great passion, but he seems to have expected Judith to be his saviour, to save him from a life spent searching for something that always eluded him; and of course he was disappointed and took some time to recover, if we read between the lines of Cosima's diary. The qualities of his Psyche in Scorpio were necessary for him to have a love life that brought him joy and growth, but he certainly had great difficulty in developing them due to the early deaths of his first two Cupids.

The life and work of Richard Wagner is an important source of insight into what a close aspect between the Sun and the asteroid Psyche in the birth chart may reflect: a crucial influence of the relationship with the father, or lack of it, in the subject's life. This relationship is necessary to reveal the qualities of Psyche, and these qualities are necessary for solar fulfilment. The solar chart of Richard Wagner's father-in-law, his "father Geyer" born on 21 January 1779, shows he would have been a good projective support for the qualities of Scorpio, since he has an exact Sun-Pluto conjunction, and Mars and Saturn are in Scorpio. His Psyche was sextile that of his son-in-law. This relationship could have replaced the one that failed to develop with his father, and Geyer could have served as Cupid, a spur for Wagner to develop the qualities of his Psyche in Scorpio. But he died too soon, and Wagner's unconscious memory also retained traces of the loss of his biological father. Death deprived Wagner of the relationship he needed. A terribly high expectation of the relationship with his father led to disillusionment and disappointment, and to a longing for salvation, for redemption, which he feared was impossible.

Friedrich Nietzsche

The chart of the philosopher, whose very special relationship with Wagner has already been mentioned previously, is also of particular interest. In Nietzsche's chart, Psyche squares the Sun, with an orb of 3°47. In Nietzsche's family, the pastorate was passed from father to son: both his grandfathers and his father were pastors. But Nietzsche lost his father, who died after a bad fall when he was only five years old. Unlike Wagner, Nietzsche had known his father and remembered how much he admired him, spending hours watching him work in his study.

In 1864, following in his father's footsteps, he entered the University of Bonn to study theology. Although he participated in student life, he felt uncomfortable in this environment and spent the holidays alone. In terms of our study of Psyche, Nietzsche's long hesitation about his future profession is significant: his mother and family tradition obliged him to continue with theology, but many other subjects attracted him. Gradually he settled on philology, which he studied in Leipzig. This broke his mother's heart, but she supported her son throughout his life. In reality, Nietzsche had lost his faith. A brilliant student, he obtained a professorship in philology and began to teach and write about his favourite subjects: Homer, Socrates and Greek tragedy. But at the age of 37, Nietzsche felt the need to confront Christianity.

In *The Gay Science*, he takes the superiority of the Greeks for granted: "Only when you repent does God have mercy on you' - to a Greek, that is an object of ridicule and annoyance."[44] In a break with Greek antiquity, "The Christian decision to find the world ugly and bad has made the world ugly and bad." We can't help but think of Freud and the symbolic desire to kill the father when we read Nietzsche's comments on Christianity and, more strikingly, on priests. In *On the Genealogy of Morals*, in 1887, he asserts: "Priests, it is well known, are the most malicious enemies – why is that? Because they are the most incapable. Impotence makes them grow a monstrous, sinister, intellectual and venomous hatred." He continues in *The Antichrist*, driving the nail in further: "The vicious being par excellence is the priest: he teaches against nature. Against the priest, it is no longer reasons that are needed, but prison."

---

44 Friedrich Nietzsche. *The Gay Science* (Cambridge University Press 2001).

It's also interesting to note the following sentence, also from *The Antichrist*: "It is essential that we say who we experience as our opposite: theologians and everything that has the blood of theologians in its veins." Nietzsche feels obliged to specify who his opposite is. And his opposite is the man who has chosen the same life as his father, who carries out the same mission. He is, in truth, his father. Of course, the expression "to have the blood of a theologian in one's veins" is to be taken figuratively, but it's significant that Nietzsche had, in a literal sense, the blood of a theologian in his veins. The problem of identity is thus underlined once again in a person with a Sun-Psyche aspect in his birth chart.

For Wagner, the absence of a relationship with a father led to a series of tragedies in which the question of the father's identity or death is central, showing the depth of the absence felt. For Nietzsche, the absence of a relationship with a father seems to have driven him to create a post-mortem relationship in which the son rebels against the father, fights him, denies him, even hates him. But in this relationship, one of the protagonists is no longer there to interact or defend himself. In his last work, *Ecce Homo*, before his descent into madness, he continued his struggle as if trying to get a reaction from a father he'd always missed: "Christian morality is the worst form of the will to lie, it is the true Circe of humanity: it is what has corrupted it." While Wagner was trying to shed light on a father who remained unknown and alien to him, Nietzsche was convinced he'd shed light for the rest of humanity on men like his father, those who believe and, worse still, are priests.

His relationship with Wagner was, by his own admission, the most important relationship of Nietzsche's life. He treated him as he'd treated his own father: at first admired, even adored, he was rejected, and Nietzsche spent the rest of his life denouncing the alleged Wagnerian imposture. As we've seen, the break was completed in the year when the progressed Sun was sextile Psyche. Wagner's death came five years later, but it didn't quell Nietzsche's hatred. In 1888, before sinking into madness, he wrote (or completed) *The Wagner Case, Twilight of the Idols, The Antichrist, Ecce Homo* and *Nietzsche contra Wagner*. In January 1889, he began sending letters that suggested he'd slipped into another reality. One of his closest friends found him curled up on his sofa in the dark, the proofs of *Nietzsche contra Wagner* in front of him. The essay had been published only two weeks before and he'd sunk into madness. Of course, Nietzsche's health had been a source of concern for years: migraines, unbearable eye pain. But the fact he took leave of his senses after dealing two fatal blows to his former idol is significant.

In *The Case of Wagner*, he'd written: "Is Wagner a man at all? Is he not rather a disease? Everything he touches he contaminates. He has made music sick." This is the same hatred he had for priests. In *Nietzsche contra Wagner*, he again defines who his opposite is: "The following chapters [...] read consecutively, can leave no one in any doubt, either concerning myself, or concerning Wagner: we are antipodes." Thus, as we have seen, his opposite is the theologian, and now his antipode is Wagner. His two fathers are what he sees as his anti-self, and he seems to be able to gain a sense of identity by stating who he is not. And yet he writes that Wagner was the relationship of his life: "For I had no one save Richard Wagner." Once again, a close natal aspect between the asteroid Psyche and the Sun seems to reflect a predisposition to see the relationship with the father, or his substitute, as central and decisive in one's life.

In the philosopher's chart, Psyche is in Capricorn, conjunct Saturn in the second house. His father and Wagner were born in the same year: they both had Saturn in Capricorn and therefore possessed a part of Capricorn's beauty which interested Nietzsche most: of Saturn. Nietzsche had to distinguish himself from his paternal models, both to embody the father himself, the leader in terms of values (second house) and to assume his position as a philosopher-hermit in a sought-after solitude. He had to develop the qualities of Capricorn to satisfy his Venus in Virgo, ruler of the Sun in Libra. Being in earth signs, they share certain values, and the philosophical purity sought by this Venus in Virgo in the ninth house could draw on the talents Nietzsche developed in Capricornian solitude and independence. Venus is in square to the nodal axis of the Moon, which is superimposed on the ascendant-descendant axis. Any planet squaring the nodal axis is destined to play a major role in the life of the individual. Here we see how everything seems to come together to make the relationship in general, and the relationship with the father in particular, the central node of Nietzsche's life: the Sun in Libra squaring Psyche and Saturn, Venus, the ruler of the Sun, squaring the nodal axis (and the Moon), the nodal axis on the ascendant-descendant axis. Even the Scorpio ascendant underlines the relational stakes.

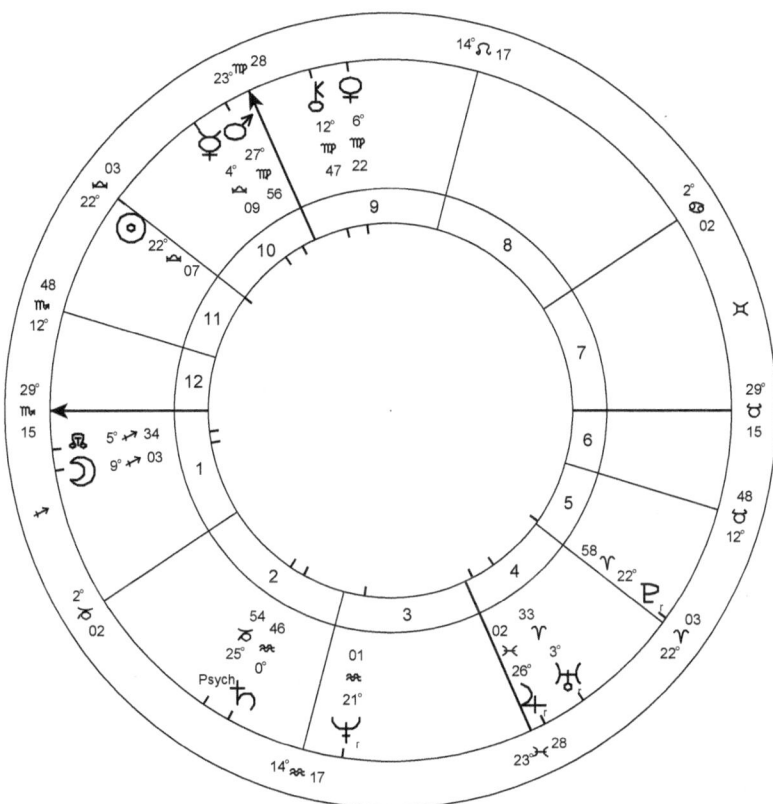

In Nietzsche's chart, the Sun is closely opposite Pluto and, more broadly, square Saturn. With Psyche in square to the Sun at birth, the philosopher felt a tension: he needed to find divine beauty in his father in order to generate the desire and longing necessary to reveal Psyche's qualities, but the luminary's aspects to Pluto and Saturn gave him the impression that he needed to free himself from the influence of his father in order to be an individual. From then on, he felt the need to reject the father and what he embodied. Psyche falls in love with the beauty of her divine lover; for Nietzsche, this is much more ambiguous. If Wagner is anything to go by, the square suggests an alternating phase of deification of the father or his substitute, with a phase of rejection and denigration. One thing is certain: the end of the relationship with Wagner, at the time when the progressed Sun was sextile Psyche, allowed Nietzsche to embody the Psyche-Saturn conjunction in the second house.

In his case, whenever Psyche is at stake, either through the transit of a planet on the natal asteroid, or through Psyche's return, or through the arrival of a planet in progression, Saturn is also activated. For Nietzsche, relationships were often the source of the disappointment necessary to encourage him to return to his hermit position and reflect, think, alone, without being contaminated by the thoughts of others or by his own feelings. As he himself said in a letter to his friend Mathilde Maier: "I live in solitude – for years, if need be – until, matured and complete as a philosopher of life, I can associate with people."

From letters written by his mother during the ten years that she cared for her mad son, we learn he played Wagner on the piano and enjoyed listening to it. Mrs Nietzsche also writes that he spoke to her at least once about the Bible, saying he'd read it in its entirety in 1888, and he seemed to speak of it as a convinced Christian. Of course, this isn't really Nietzsche anymore, but he seemed to have made peace with his father, the pastor, and with his surrogate father, Wagner. Even if we don't value what he did in the last ten years of his life, we can only conclude that his career, his intellectual life and his philosophical production ended with *Nietzsche contra Wagner*, where he stated: "Illness is always the answer, whenever we venture to doubt our right to our mission, whenever we begin to make things too easy for ourselves." Perhaps Nietzsche was tired of fighting his father and his surrogate, and simply wanted to "make things too easy". Illness became the answer.

Finally, we've seen that the theme of the prohibition against revealing one's identity is central to two of Wagner's operas. Nietzsche, in the epilogue to *Nietzsche contra Wagner*, seems to affirm the choice not to do as Psyche did: to let what is veiled remain unknown, not to pretend to have access to the truth. It's worth noting that this was one of the last texts he wrote: "We shall scarcely be found on the track of those Egyptian youths who break into temples at night, who embrace statues, and would fain unveil, strip, and set in broad daylight, everything which there are excellent reasons to keep concealed." And he added, in French: *"tout comprendre, c'est tout mépriser"* (to understand everything is to despise everything). At the end of his life, therefore, Nietzsche thought he'd shone his oil lamp on his father and Wagner, which had led him to despise them. He seemed to regret this and to believe that certain secrets must remain. In astrological terms, Nietzsche went in search of the beauty evoked by the asteroid Psyche, believing it belonged first to his father and then to Wagner. In the end, he was able to make the Capricorn beauty of his Psyche his own, but in doing so, he burdened himself with the solitude he needed and, above all, with the contempt he felt for his idols.

Pierre

Another significant example is that of a client of mine whose Sun and Psyche form a square of 1°30 orb. He came to see me at the instigation of his wife because he felt "trapped" in his father's life since his death. His father had bought a listed house, which he'd been restoring for some twenty years, and Pierre wanted to buy out his sisters' shares in order to continue their father's work. This worried his wife, who feared they would "bury themselves" there. Her husband had also positioned himself as the head of the family, which was scattered over France, organising family reunions himself, trying to bring together his father's children and grandchildren, as well as his cousins.

At the mention of his father, he couldn't hide his admiration, gratitude and love. He said he'd inherited his values, knowledge, courage and faith from him. He couldn't remember ever rebelling against his father because he'd always seen him as a role model, even as a teenager. Here we see one of the possible manifestations of his natal Sun-Chiron square: an unattainable, almost untouchable father who makes the little boy doubt his right to develop his Sun. But Psyche brings additional information: the first image of divine beauty was seen in the father. This quality belonged to Pierre, but in order to make it his own, he thought it necessary to resemble his father in every way. Since Cupid was perfect, to be worthy of him he had to be perfect. His Psyche in Gemini forms a 1° T-square with his father's Jupiter in Sagittarius and Chiron in Pisces. These two signs are concerned with the religious or spiritual, and much of Pierre's admiration for his father came from seeing him as almost a saint, a model, a guide for his faith.

Unlike Wagner and Nietzsche, he hadn't lost his father when he was a child. On the contrary, he'd been close to him throughout his childhood, even though his father worked a lot and Pierre saw little of him. As an adult, Pierre had continued to see him twice a month, even after moving to another city, and had spent three weeks of his annual holidays with him. He didn't lose him until he was fifty. But the importance of his father in his choices and values made it by far the most important relationship in his life. The construction of his identity (the Sun) was based on the values and opinions his father passed on to him. One might think that his father was very authoritarian and left his eldest son little choice. Admittedly, like many men of his generation (born before the First World War), it wouldn't have occurred to him to adapt his upbringing to his children's personalities, and for him patriotic values, those of a man who had fought in the war, were essential to a boy's education. But above all, he was a loving father who would never have asked Pierre to carry such a heavy burden on his shoulders. Not only did he want to continue his father's life after his death, but even after fifty years, Pierre was still comparing himself to him, and this comparison was always to his detriment: his father was more honest, more physically resistant, more intelligent, a better father, etc.

What Wagner, Nietzsche and Pierre have in common is the importance of the father in the construction of the individual and the fact he remained, into adulthood, a standard by which the subject continued to judge himself. All three were born with a predisposition to see divine beauty in the father, and needed the relationship with the father (Sun-Psyche), or a substitute, in order to honour Venus and find their sense of worth. For Wagner, it is doubt and the attraction of the mystery of identity that dominate, because the father is totally unknown. For Nietzsche, the theologian, i.e. the father, is his opposite, the one who receives his hatred but allows him to appropriate Psyche in Capricorn. For Pierre, the father is the true embodiment of divine beauty, an unattainable model whose work he believes he can only try to continue.

John Lennon

John Lennon had an exact trine between the Sun and Psyche in his birth chart. He seems to have rejected any form of paternal symbol or surrogate throughout his life: he embodied the archetypal rebel, calling for the rejection of existing social models and religions. In his song "God", released at the time of the quincunx between his progressed Sun and Psyche, he said he no longer believed in The Beatles, Bob Dylan (Zimmerman), kings, Jesus, Kennedy or Elvis, but only in himself and Yoko. All his idols and the men who could have been a father to him are rejected out of hand. His real father abandoned him after divorcing his mother when Lennon was five. His chart shows a Sun-Mars conjunction in Sagittarius, the midpoint of which is exactly opposite his son's Psyche at 16°17 Gemini. Raised by his aunt and uncle, John also lost his uncle, who died when he was fifteen. This "adoptive father" uncle presented a grand cross in mutable signs aspecting Lennon's Psyche: Pluto conjunct the latter at 17°42 Gemini, Uranus at 25°30 Sagittarius, the Sun at 21°45 in Pisces and the Moon in Virgo (we don't have the time of birth, but it's opposite the Sun for most of the day). The beauty Lennon perceived in his father was coloured by the Sun and Mars, and in his uncle by Pluto, the Sun and Uranus. Both embodied a certain kind of power, masculinity, to which Lennon's uncle added the ability to transform things and people, and to embody a certain freedom, perhaps against the flow. But this beauty was probably something overwhelming for the little boy and the young teenager in both cases, especially in the case of the uncle, Pluto being the planet closely conjunct Psyche. Lennon certainly admired this man, but he rejected him and very quickly rebelled against him, because to appropriate Cupid's beauty required him to make that power and solar radiation his own. Lennon needed this relationship to build a sense of self and develop his core identity, but the tensions between his Psyche and his uncle's chart prevented him from simply appropriating this beauty, like Margaret Thatcher, whom we will discuss below. As always with Psyche, the asteroid can't be interpreted without considering the chart as a whole: Lennon presented a conjunction at the same degree of Taurus between Jupiter and Saturn, in quincunx to the Sun, and the theme of the dethronement of the king, if we refer to Hesiod's *Theogony*, comes through strongly. The fact Psyche is in exact trine to the Sun reinforces paternal issues because of the need to find beauty in a paternal model, even if it's to make it one's own by dethroning the model. So he spent part of his life searching for a leader to admire.

As a teenager, he thought he was a genius that no one had discovered, while at the same time fearing he was mad.[45] He wanted to be the next Elvis, and wrote poetry and drew pictures, but he was violent and often got into fights. Lennon was violent for a long time, including to his first

---

45 Jann S. Wenner, *Lennon Remembers: The Full Rolling Stone Interviews from 1970* (New York: Verso, 2000).

wife Cynthia, and terrifying to his first son Julian. He was constantly rebellious, but couldn't find a cause to commit himself to. Lennon rejected the Father more as a symbol of authority, morality, tradition and country rather than his father in particular or people like him, as Nietzsche had done. He married a Japanese woman and left Liverpool to live with her in New York, and he took a lot of drugs, including heroin, which had serious consequences for him and The Beatles. Lennon campaigned for non-violence in the midst of the Vietnam War and for African American civil rights. He also made experimental albums with Yoko Ono, one of which had a cover showing them completely naked. He made short films with his wife, which were sometimes praised, sometimes booed, so disturbing and innovative were they. One in particular follows the path of a fly on the naked body of a sleeping woman. On their honeymoon, Lennon and Ono received journalists naked under the sheets in their hotel room.

The exact trine between Lennon's Sun and Psyche doesn't mean his father would abandon him or that John wouldn't tolerate authority. But Lennon was born with a disposition that would make the relationship with his father the most important in the construction of his identity (Sun) and self-esteem (Venus), for divine beauty was supposed to belong to the father principle. Lennon then pursued this beauty through various substitutes, all of which proved disappointing and inadequate. The song "God", written at the time of the break-up with McCartney, marked a turning point for him: according to the lyrics, he was no longer looking for a father, a model or a god in Dylan, Elvis, Buddha, Jesus, Kennedy or The Beatles. Lennon initially felt great admiration for some of the people mentioned in "God", before rejecting them: The Beatles (i.e. McCartney), Dylan and JFK. Lennon had admired Dylan for years before feeling compelled to knock him off his pedestal. McCartney, as we've seen in Part Three, had Mercury conjunct John's Psyche and the Sun, Saturn and Uranus in Gemini. Dylan was marked by the same sign, in which he had a stellium composed of the Sun, Venus and Mercury. His Venus is lined up within 3° of John's Psyche. JFK was also marked by the same sign, with the Sun and Venus at the same degree as Lennon's Psyche. When Lennon was asked who he admired, Neil Young was often the first name mentioned. He had Uranus at 16°27 Gemini. Lennon worked with Elton John and David Bowie, both of whom had Uranus at about 18° of the same sign. All these men embodied something of the beauty of Gemini, which attracted Lennon like a magnet. The inspirational figures of Young, Elton John and Bowie had their Uranus conjunct Lennon's Psyche and served to awaken his buried Geminian qualities: his love of freedom, his eclecticism, his adaptability and his taste for relationships. In fact, Bowie wasn't blind to John's Gemini qualities and had told him so when he said he loved his use of puns, which were extremely good, and his sense of humour was unique.

Finally, when his progressed Moon hit Psyche, two years before his death, Lennon hired a personal assistant, Frederic Seaman. Seaman wrote a book about the years he spent working with Lennon, who was then a stay-at-home dad and starting to compose again. Seaman was instrumental in making Lennon feel secure, while also serving as his confidante and giving him a renewed desire to create. Seaman had a Sun-Saturn conjunction in Libra, 1° from John's Sun and therefore in trine to John's Psyche. Seaman's Psyche was also trine John's. So the very month his progressed Moon was conjunct his Psyche, John felt the need to enter into a new relationship in his life, evoking the sign of Gemini and the symbol of the twins to establish a daily companionship that would help him emotionally and creatively.

Thus, with an exact Sun-Psyche trine, the asteroid played a major role in Lennon's life, in his choice of models, friends and people with whom he created. The moment of the quincunx between his progressed Sun and Psyche was particularly decisive: he followed his primal therapy and broke with McCartney, and set about multiplying the encounters and collaborations necessary to develop the qualities of his Psyche in Gemini – and by the same token, those of his Venus in Virgo and his Sun in Libra. He succeeded in leaving behind the image of the rebel who rejects established structures out of hand, to become a man committed to fighting injustice and promoting peace. He was able to become an awakener who denounced inequalities. The virtues of Gemini were essential for him to be true to himself and to nourish his art, his personality and his commitments.

Margaret Thatcher

Margaret Thatcher, whose Sun in Libra was trine Psyche in Gemini with an orb of 5°14, allows us to study the effects of aspects between the Luminary and the asteroid in a woman's life. After being appointed Prime Minister in 1979, Thatcher told the press: "I just owe almost everything to my own father. I really do. He brought me up to believe all the things that I do believe and they're just the values on which I've fought the Election. And it's passionately interesting for me that the things that I learned in a small town, in a very modest home, are just the things that I believe have won the Election."

Her father was Thatcher's first supporter, the first to believe she could be anything other than a housewife. But Alfred Robert wasn't a man in a position to give her a start, or to pay for her expensive studies at the best English universities. The son and grandson of shoemakers, he'd wanted to be a teacher but had left school at thirteen because he had no money to pay for his education, so he became a grocer. He met Margaret's mother, a seamstress, at the local Methodist church, where they were married in 1917. As they were very thrifty, they were able to buy their own grocery shop, above which the whole family settled. Although Thatcher explains in her memoirs that living above the shop meant living with the customers, who could disturb the family at any time of the day or night, she acknowledges it also meant having the chance to see her parents much more than other children. She had the opportunity to share every meal with her parents and to develop a real relationship with her father. In her memoirs she recalls: "We had much more time to talk than some other families, for which I have always been grateful."[46]

Much is made in her memoirs of her father's influence on her future choices. She emphasises the importance of Methodism in her family and her father becoming a much sought-after lay preacher whose sermons were admired by his daughter. She describes a man who was intelligent and cultured despite his leaving school early, and that he was serious, reliable, honest and rigorous: a man of principle. He used to tell her: "Never do things just because other people do them." Thatcher added that, for her, "the sentiment stood me in good stead, as it did my father." She goes on to add: "These upright qualities, which entailed a refusal to alter your convictions just because others disagreed or because you became unpopular, were instilled into me from the earliest days." Thatcher was unpopular on more than one occasion, as were her decisions. But she never sought to change what she believed to be right in the light of public opinion, earning her the label of inflexible from her detractors and honest from her admirers. In any case, she followed her father's example.

---

46 Margaret Thatcher, *The Path to Power* (HarperCollins 1995).

Talking about her family's opinions as a child, she says: "we had our own views about that in the Roberts household [...] being staunchly Conservative, we were the odd family out."[47] The subject is the vote for peace organised by the Methodists before the Second World War, in 1935. What is interesting is "in the Roberts household" as if, even at the age of ten, her father's opinions were her own. Her respect for her father is palpable: "his leisure and entertainment always seemed to merge into duty" or: "The Rotary motto, 'Service Above Self', was engraved on his heart." Margaret Thatcher was an educated woman, unlike her mother, and here too she owed something to her father. According to her memoirs: "I was probably reading more widely than most of my classmates, doubtless through my father's influence, and it showed on occasion." Thatcher thought it was a form of revenge because her father hadn't received the education he'd have liked. He liked to talk to her about what she'd read at school. Every week he borrowed a novel from the library for his wife and a "serious" book to share with Margaret. He soon discovered she was most interested in books on politics and international affairs. One day he noticed she didn't know the poet Whitman. He was quick to remedy the situation, and she added to the anecdote in her memoirs that Whitman remained one of her favourite authors.

As well as giving his daughter a solid general education, Alfred Robert introduced her to politics "on the ground", having added to his job as a grocer the roles of town councillor, deputy finance minister, first deputy mayor and, finally, mayor of his town, he introduced her to many of his contacts and to a large number of important events. But he insisted that politics had its limits, which would become one of Thatcher's creeds. He believed in personal responsibility and fiscal rigour: here again we see what made Thatcherism so special. Finally, Thatcher owed her interest in the law to her father: married with children and out of work, she began to study law. In her memoirs she says: "As with my fascination with politics, it was my father who had been responsible for stimulating this interest."

We have seen that an aspect between the Sun and Psyche highlights the place of the father in the individual's life, values, and choices. In Thatcher's case this is a trine, and the father seems to have played a crucial role in the unveiling of his daughter's Geminian qualities. What's more, Thatcher's

---

47 Margaret Thatcher, *The Path to Power* (HarperCollins 1995).

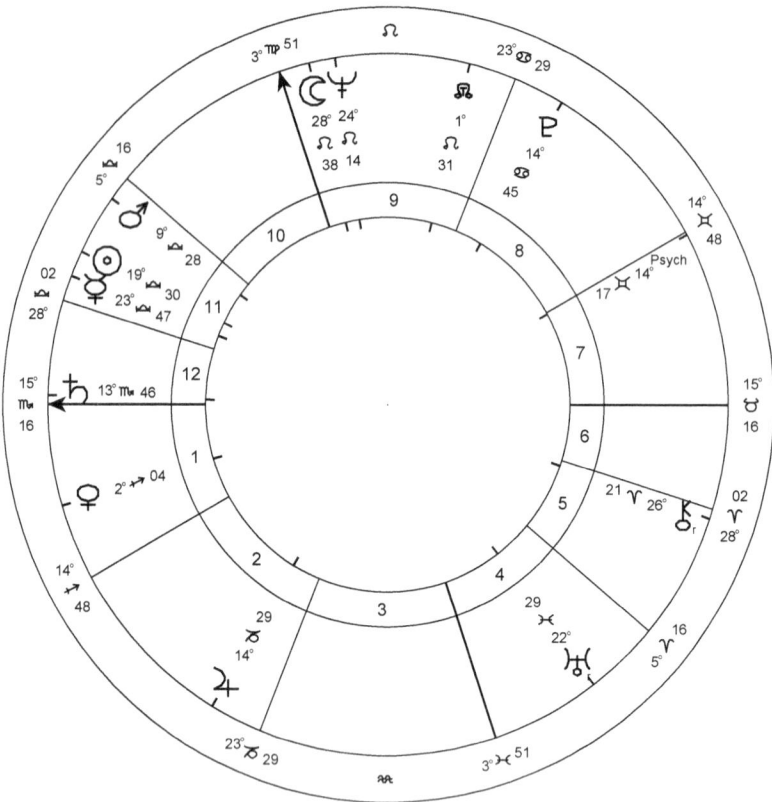

Psyche is conjunct her father's Venus at 14°17 and 13°57 Gemini, respectively. Her father had a stellium in Gemini made up of Venus, Pluto and Neptune. Being marked by the sign of Gemini, he made it easy for his daughter to see the beauty of the sign and to search for it within herself. Thatcher was born with a predisposition to see divine beauty in her father, a set of eminently desirable qualities that she was destined to make her own. So she was extremely fortunate that her father did everything he could to share his Geminian gifts and pass them on to her, making her task much easier. First of all, he gave his daughter freedom and allowed her to acquire a very good general culture and education. He gave her the habit of debating and speaking in front of large audiences, and he also gave her his values: Methodism, rigour, honesty, individual freedom and responsibility.

In Thatcher's chart, Psyche is quincunx Saturn, with an orb of 0°31. As with Nietzsche, the relationship with her father was a necessary means of revealing her Saturnian qualities, which were more than brought to the fore in her role as Prime Minister.

The myth of Psyche invites us to look at Venus. In this chart, she's in Sagittarius and ruler of the Sun in Libra. There's no doubt the paternal attitude was very supportive for both his daughter's Psyche in Gemini and Venus in Sagittarius, for Thatcher derived much pleasure from sharing her father's passions: law, politics and religion. These themes are dear to Sagittarius because they are linked to the way we live together and to the formation of social groups. Venus is in the first house and thus describes the family atmosphere in early childhood. In this house, the planet is easily recognised as ours, as an important part of our personality. By taking such an interest in her, her father undoubtedly gave her the confidence she needed to try so many things, and encouraged the natural expression of such a Venus, who derives her joy from sharing collective values. Thatcher was able to reveal the qualities of her Gemini Psyche thanks to her father, who she believed possessed them and who allowed her to feel the desire to make them her own. These qualities were necessary for Venus, but also – and this is emphasised by the natal trine – for the Sun. She therefore needed to unveil the wisdom of Gemini to feel that her life had meaning. Her political ambition was fuelled above all by the sense of having an important role to play and the certainty of being unique. In the case of a Sun-Psyche trine, the relationship with the father is likely to produce these feelings, if the father shows the child the qualities he desires and helps them to acquire them.

Madame du Châtelet and Camille Claudel

Sun-Psyche aspects, considered 'favourable' or at least facilitating by traditional astrology, are also in the charts of two other women who were brilliantly successful, at times and in fields where almost no other woman could excel. In both cases, the father played a decisive role: Madame du Châtelet, mentioned earlier, and Camille Claudel, the sculptor. In the case of Émilie du Châtelet, there was a 3° trine between the Sun in Sagittarius and Psyche in Leo. For Camille Claudel, there was a 3°19 sextile between the Sun in Sagittarius and Psyche in Aquarius.

Châtelet's father, ensured there was, as previously said, little difference in the education of his sons and daughter: he gave Émilie lessons in mathematics and metaphysics, because he could see these subjects appealed to her. She received a broad education in languages, science and philosophy, which enabled her to become the great translator and excellent scientist we know. In addition to the education she received from her father, it was above all her father's approval, his tacit consent to deviate from the beaten path and the destiny of women at that time, that made the Baron de Breteuil such an exemplary and decisive father in his daughter's life. In the Claudel family, it was also the father, Louis-Prosper, who paid particular attention to his daughter (as well as to his son). On the advice of his friend Alfred Boucher, a famous sculptor, he moved the family to Paris so his daughter could benefit from an artistic education. As women were not yet allowed to sit the entrance examinations to the École des Beaux-Arts, Camille had to take lessons in private Parisian studios. Again, her father supported her. After all, at that time women, even those trained in sculpture, didn't make a career out of it: it was very much frowned upon, especially if you were doing nudes, as Camille Claudel was. Again, it took her father's encouragement and support to allow her to overcome these obstacles and finally join the Colarossi studio, then Auguste Rodin's studio.

Margaret Thatcher, Emilie du Châtelet and Camille Claudel all had high expectations of their fathers, as shown by the aspects between their Suns and Psyches, and they were fortunate their fathers valued their quest for inner truth by supporting their choices. The labours set by Venus are more likely to be successful if one has such help. In these last three cases, the father provided the impetus that directed the careers and ultimately the lives of these women, for it's impossible to separate career from life in these extraordinary destinies. Could the opposition or square reflect a more ambiguous paternal influence?

Jackie Kennedy

Jacqueline Bouvier, the future wife of John F. Kennedy and then Aristotle Onassis, was born at the moment of a close opposition, 1°, between the Sun and the asteroid. Jacqueline is an interesting case for the study of the Sun-Psyche aspects in a woman, because her love life is known to us, at least for the most part. If divine beauty is first glimpsed in the father, in adulthood it's sought in solar surrogates: a husband or lover, for these men were both her Cupids and projective supports for her solar qualities, at a time when women had few opportunities to make their own choices. One can read in some places that Jackie married her father, choosing John Fitzgerald, who was as fickle as the man who had given birth to her. But it's much more complex than that: certainly, having adored her father, she was looking for a husband whom she could also admire and love, and whom she would forgive everything. But in choosing JFK, she was also looking for a place in high society and to satisfy her excessive taste for luxury and money. She wanted to ensure she'd never run out of money and end up like her father. Because of her experience with her father, she also saw a husband as a means of ensuring an expensive lifestyle and ironclad security. But Jackie wasn't happily married to either JFK or her second husband, Onassis. Her Psyche was in Aquarius and her Venus in Gemini, two air signs that can't tolerate a union in which the woman is dependent on her husband and relegated to being merely beautiful and cultured, even if she is the First Lady of the United States. Her father, because of the natal Sun-Psyche aspect in Jackie's chart, was who she expected to show her the qualities of Aquarius and allow her to make them her own. But unlike Thatcher's father, he didn't help her at all: she expected him to show her how to be independent, to break out of the conventional role assigned to women of her time, and to allow her to see from above, which would have enabled her to understand the elements at play in a love relationship. But her father's behaviour made her associate these qualities with selfishness, danger and insecurity.

Born into a very wealthy family, Jacqueline heard her parents constantly arguing, not only about her father's infidelities but also about money. She was brought up in a very privileged environment. Her parents' Manhattan apartment had fourteen rooms and her mother had a large household staff. During the summer she lived with the Bouviers, her father's family, in Lasata, in a fifteen-room house decorated in the best English and French styles. She began her education at a school on East End Avenue, where she met other children of high society. But Jackie's situation was far less secure than it appeared. Her father, Jack Bouvier, was a stockbroker, then an independent broker, but he was also a big spender and often had debts to pay. He was a very poor manager: he made a lot of money but was incapable of not spending it immediately. He was also an inveterate gambler who bet on the races and especially on poker and frequented casinos. This less than ideal husband drank heavily and was a compulsive seducer. He began cheating on Janet, Jackie's mother, with a sixteen-year-old girl on their honeymoon. The Crash of 1929 didn't ruin him, but it forced him to cut back on his lifestyle. Unfortunately, he learned nothing from this and continued to gamble, losing heavily at poker and making bad deals. He was in debt, including to the IRS. It was then he had to tell Janet and cut back on their lifestyle. Janet, who had put up with her husband's numerous – and barely concealed – infidelities, couldn't bear to be deprived of a lifestyle to which she'd become accustomed and which was indispensable to her. Divorce was inevitable.

The separation of Jacqueline's parents was particularly cruel for the child: her parents criticised each other in her presence and Janet exposed Jack's inconsistencies. Jackie, however, always sided with her father. Janet was a strict disciplinarian, regularly resorting to slaps and punishments, because she wanted only one thing: for her daughters to be able to move freely in high society by giving them a perfect education. Black Jack, on the other hand, was only interested in winning his daughters' love, which was the only thing he could get in the end. He pampered them and encouraged them, and Jacqueline was, by all accounts, his favourite. It's true she was a particularly precocious child with obvious intellectual gifts. But she also looked a lot like him: the same thick black hair, wide-set eyes, pale complexion and facial features. During the divorce proceedings, her father's infidelities were leaked to the press and Jackie was humiliated. She didn't blame her father. In fact, she never seemed to hold a grudge against him: when he didn't turn up for her wedding to JFK because he'd been drinking the night before, she blamed her mother for excluding him from the pre-wedding dinner that evening. She wrote him a heartfelt letter explaining she knew the pressure he was under and in her mind he'd still walked her down the aisle. There were rumours that Jackie's mother had sent two friends to her ex-husband's hotel to get him drunk. It's hard to separate the true from the false, but one thing is certain: Jack Bouvier wasn't at his daughter's wedding, and she didn't hold it against him in the slightest.

After the divorce was finalised, Janet married Hugh D. Auchincloss, a stockbroker who was immensely wealthy. Jackie spent her teenage years in even more luxurious surroundings than those of her childhood. But what a contrast when she visited her father! Sure, she was treated like a princess, and she preferred him to her mother. But he had only a two-room flat, and the three of them had to live in it when she came with her sister. Alcohol had become his refuge, and he tried in vain to give it up, going through several rehabs. He continued to multiply his conquests, never trying to hide them from his daughters. He had other children, twins, whom he didn't recognise because their mother was married. He even shared women with JFK, his son-in-law, in the same evening.

What did Jacqueline take away from her relationship with her father? First, there was the fear that, like her mother, she could lose everything overnight. She had to find someone wealthy, ambitious and intelligent enough to pay for her increasingly expensive lifestyle. Her father's infidelities also left her with the ability to put up with her husband's. But if a woman in the 1950s often had to accept that her husband could be unfaithful without her having the right to do so, it seems clear that Jackie accepted far more than any other woman would have done. John Fitzgerald Kennedy cheated on her compulsively, but he also mistreated her emotionally: for example, on the day she gave birth to a stillborn child, it was Robert Kennedy, her brother-in-law, who came to her bedside, as John was in no hurry to end his stay on a yacht in Europe with beautiful women. What's more, he didn't confide in Jackie: he told her nothing of the plans he was working out with his father, Joe. The truth was that JFK didn't love her, and perhaps didn't appreciate her. She was just a well-educated, intelligent and distinguished woman who helped him improve his image. It was his father, Joe Kennedy, with his infallible instinct, who had chosen her, not him. Why did Jackie stay with him? Why did she fall in love with such a man?

On the day of Jacqueline's birth, the Sun made a very close opposition to the asteroid Psyche, indicating that the relationship with the father would be important in allowing her to express the Venusian function in a healthy way, by developing the qualities symbolised by Psyche. The opposition also suggests this relationship could be the source of ambivalent feelings or even trauma. Jackie was born with the expectation she would find divine beauty in her father and try to make it her own. But whether her father was responsible or simply a victim of circumstance, he showed her an image of beauty that was intimately linked to insecurity and irresponsibility. His daughter's Psyche in Aquarius couldn't be nurtured by Cupid's beauty: on the contrary, it may have made her more afraid of her independence and freedom. It also made her continue to seek beauty in men who treated her like her father, and to be unhappy in love for much of her life. She couldn't hold a grudge against her father or question him because, with the natal Sun-Psyche aspect, he embodied the beauty she sought. Her Psyche was at 6°17 Aquarius, exactly trine her father's Neptune at 6°11 Gemini, and also closely trine her father's Pluto (7°09) and North Node (5°23) in Gemini. The father's beauty was therefore coloured by Neptune, which explains why his daughter idealised him but was often disappointed by him, and why he seemed so elusive. His beauty was also coloured by Pluto, reflecting the insecurity inherent in the relationship, as if something threatening were in the air. With JFK, she thought she was rediscovering the beauty she'd glimpsed in her father, with her Psyche closely trine his Sun at 7°52 in Gemini, opposite his Neptune at 2°40 Leo, and quincunx Pluto at 3°16 Cancer. JFK thus allowed her to replace her father as Cupid, the bearer of the same divine Gemini-Neptune-Pluto beauty. She relived the boundless admiration for a man who had disappointed her so much, and the constant feeling of insecurity, partly because of his infidelities, but also because he never revealed himself to her and remained partly an unknown. It should be added that JFK had a Sun-Psyche square in his chart, suggesting the couple had similar father issues.

Jackie compensated for her insecurity as best she could. Her relationship with money was pathological, with compulsive and lavish spending. Several episodes in Jacqueline's life illustrate the need and desire for a very luxurious lifestyle, beyond reason and far above romantic feelings. Onassis, after JFK's death, was the rare gem she was looking for: much older, cultured, very self-assured and immensely rich. He regularly sent her gifts worth millions of dollars: diamonds, rubies, emeralds and pearls. He lived in Greece when he wasn't travelling on business, and she had no intention of leaving Manhattan, but she chose him. She explained she was looking for security. Her new husband gave her a budget of $550,000 a month, which she regularly exceeded. When she didn't get any extra money, she sold clothes through her personal secretary and bought more with the money she got. One day she bought two hundred pairs of shoes in one afternoon. Onassis had Chiron at 6°27 of Aquarius, lined up with Jackie's Psyche. There was also a cross aspect between Jackie's Psyche and her husband's Neptune, a 2°11 quincunx. Onassis had Psyche at 29°55 Taurus,

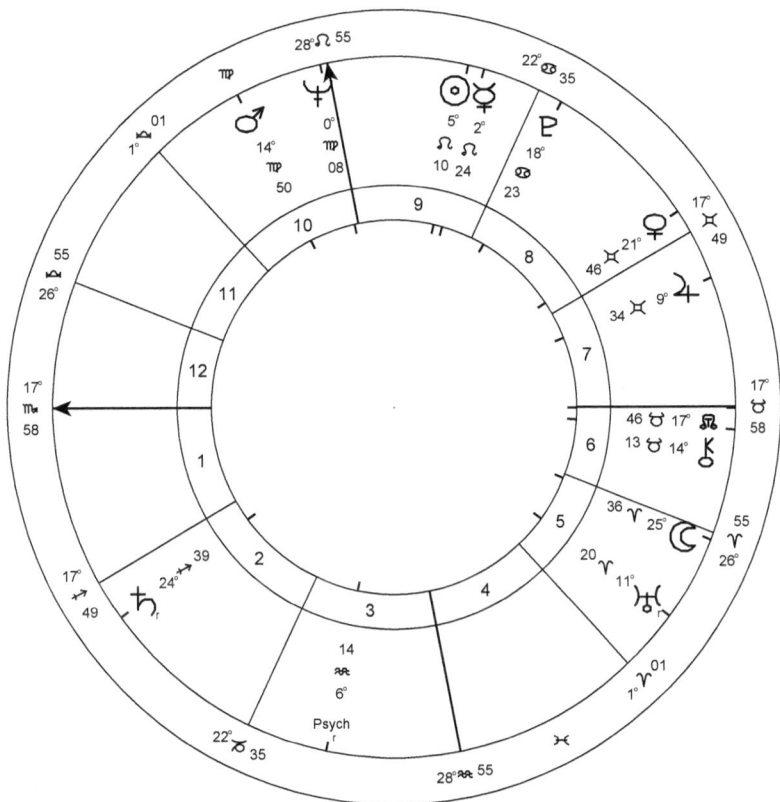

1° from Jack Bouvier's Sun, suggesting that Jacqueline may have seen the hidden beauty in Onassis that she'd loved so much in her father. Her new husband also had an exact Sun-Psyche trine, suggesting a problem similar to his wife's. She certainly sensed in him the potential to heal the wounds inflicted by her father, and the beauty of Chiron in Aquarius dazzled her enough at first for Onassis to embody her new Cupid, partly resembling her father. But as always with Chiron, we can go from the one who heals to the one who wounds, and vice versa; after the death of his son, Onassis, blaming Jackie, who seemed to bring death wherever she went, violently rejected her.

In her two marriages, Jackie fled an unstable and ruined father, but continued to seek the divine beauty she'd seen in him in her lovers.

Lacking discernment and unable to apply the Platonic virtues that the myth explains are a prerequisite for healthy relationships, her choices in love were never made according to her affinities and values. In her chart, Venus is in Gemini, in the eighth house. In her case, the planet should find pleasure in verbal exchange, shared eclectic interests and new learning. However, it was also in opposition to Saturn, and here we find the need for a reassuring husband-father. With her husbands she didn't experience the Gemini aspect of Venus, nor the deep emotional sharing that the eighth house implies. Kennedy never really enjoyed talking to her and never confided his thoughts to her. He said more to his last mistress, Mary Pinchot Meyer, to the great distress of Jackie, who was experiencing a quincunx between her progressed Sun and Psyche at the time of the affair. With Onassis, there must have been a few Gemini exchanges when he was courting her, as they were very cultured. For a good year they were quite happy together, but their cultural differences soon got the better of them, and Onassis left her, as did John, because his business kept him travelling all the time. The marriage was a disaster and once again Jackie was unhappy and spent money she didn't have.

As soon as Psyche sees Cupid, she loses him, and to find him she has to endure the labours dictated by Venus. Revealing the qualities of Psyche and honouring Venus is an obligatory point of passage from the stage when beauty is admired and desired in others, to the stage when it's discovered and cultivated in oneself. Jackie's relationship with her father, which was a mixture of love but neglect, emotional blackmail and humiliation through public debauchery, prevented a healthy expression of the planet Venus, and an early unveiling of her Psyche's qualities. In her love choices, Jackie placed little value on herself and measured her worth by the money people were prepared to spend on her. Her father adored her, of course, but he didn't take on any of his paternal responsibilities: neither material security, nor education, nor dignity. Above all, he spent far more time drinking and having affairs than with his daughters. Liz Greene sees Venus-Saturn aspects as a sign of conditional love: no free love is given to the child, and if he wants to feel loved, he has to please the parent.[48] This seems particularly true of Jackie's life: on her mother's side it's obvious. But

---

[48] Liz Greene and Howard Sasportas, *Dynamics of the Unconscious: Seminars in Psychology Astrology, Vol.2* (Red Wheel / Weiser, 1988).

she also had to make her father proud and play the role of the daughter who adored her father and never reproached him for his irresponsible behaviour. If we add to the Venus-Saturn opposition in Jacqueline's chart the Sun-Psyche opposition and the large square between Chiron and the Sun, we understand that the way her father showed his affection for her and behaved towards her had a major influence on her identity, her choices in love and her self-esteem.

Onassis's death left Jacqueline with $26 million. Widowed for the second time, Jacqueline began to date a number of men. For the first time, she was freed from the need to find a very rich man. It's possible that at this time in her life she was finally able to ask herself questions about her true identity, symbolised by the Sun, and to do so through relationships (Psyche). To quote one of her biographers, recalling the two years after Onassis's death and her love affairs: "Free from marital ties, freed, thanks to her fortune, from all preoccupation with her future, she was finally able to explore the depths of her own nature. Who is she? What does she want? What does she refuse? Where does she stand in her relationships with men? And with society in general? Instinctively, she felt tempted by these experiences which would bring her this essential good: to know herself."[49]

When Onassis died, Jackie took the time to date several men without settling down, and found a job in publishing, two ways of honouring a Venus in Gemini. Above all, the Aquarian qualities of her Psyche could finally be expressed, now she was financially independent and no longer relying on men to give her an identity. Capable of autonomy and distancing herself from her emotional problems thanks to intensive psychotherapy, she was able to use the airy virtues of Aquarius to connect with a man, this time in a genuine way. While distancing is part of the wisdom of Aquarius, its courage is of taking the risk of independence and letting go of archaic lunar needs. Once the qualities of Psyche have been integrated, relationships (Psyche) become a tool for self-awareness and for the construction of one's identity (Sun). This is the gift of a Sun-Psyche contact at birth, but it's easier to use if the father was able to present some of the divine beauty of Cupid, and the planet Venus was able to express herself. A father unable to portray Cupid's beauty or to recognise his own or his child's beauty, makes the process much more difficult.

---

49 Henry Gidel, *Jackie Kennedy* (Flammarion, 2011).

Psyche in Aspect to the Moon

In the myth, the lunar goddesses refuse to help Psyche because it's Venus, not the Moon, who must be worshipped. Aspects between the Moon and Psyche therefore might make access to Psyche more difficult than aspects between the Sun and Psyche or between Venus and Psyche. In the early life of a person with a significant Moon-Psyche aspect, the mother is the first Cupid: it's in her that the child sees divine beauty and then tries to make it their own. The child gradually becomes aware, at the same time as they separate from their mother, that this beauty does not belong to them, and this loss feeds their intra-psychic quest. If, for one reason or another, the mother is unable to support the child in their quest to appropriate the qualities of Psyche, they will seek to establish other lunar-type relationships, with maternal surrogates, to help them do so. The aim, of course, remains to honour Venus, and the qualities thus revealed must then be able to be invested in the Venusian realm.

Malcolm X

When studying a planet or an asteroid, it's particularly interesting to consider the effects of conjunction, especially when it's very close. Malcolm X, the African-American who made headlines in the 1960s by campaigning for racial segregation, was born at the moment of an exact conjunction between the Moon and Psyche. Malcolm X's childhood remains full of uncertainties because few people have spoken about this period of his life. Moreover, it's difficult to give an objective account because his personality is so divisive. We do know, however, that his father, a carpenter and Baptist preacher, died in suspicious circumstances when Malcolm was six years old; he was found run over by a tram. It was clear to family members that he'd been beaten unconscious by members of the Ku Klux Klan before being placed on the tracks. Malcolm's mother was left to look after her seven children alone, which caused her to fall into a depression and then a kind of madness that led to her being institutionalised when Malcolm was about eleven years old. She stayed there for twenty-three years.

What profoundly shaped Malcolm X's destiny was his skin colour, which was similar to that of his mother's. His father was black, as were his brothers and sisters. He and his mother, on the other hand, were much lighter, due to the mixed race of his mother, a West Indian born to a black mother and a white father. Rightly or wrongly, the family believed Malcolm's grandmother had been raped. His mother's light, mixed-race skin was therefore a symbol of rape, shame and enslavement. This was Louise's experience, and she transferred her disgust at her skin colour to Malcolm. He wrote in his autobiography that she was always harder on him than on his siblings because she wanted him to understand he had no special rights just because he looked white. Using the symbolism of a Moon-Psyche conjunction, we can assume Malcolm had a terrible need to find in himself the beauty he perceived in his mother. Their shared skin colour could have helped him to recognise himself in her and to mobilise the psychic energy needed to develop the qualities symbolised by Psyche. But instead, this commonality was a real tragedy for the child; it meant he'd inherited what his mother found ugliest in her: her origin.

During his adolescence and early adulthood, Malcolm made the most of his light skin colour to integrate: he had his hair straightened and socialised with white people, including white women, which was highly unusual in the United States. After many crises (alcohol, drugs, crime, prison, etc.), Malcolm converted to Islam and became a member of the Nation of Islam sect, which advocated segregation between Whites and Blacks, believing Whites were the incarnation of the Devil on Earth. This viewpoint was radically opposed to that of Martin Luther King, who was campaigning at the same time. Malcolm soon became the charismatic leader of the Nation of Islam, second only to its founder. He gave many speeches in which he proclaimed his hatred of Whites and his desire to establish Black supremacy, and he publicly rejoiced in the death of certain Whites. In the end, however, he was murdered by members of his sect because, towards the end of his life, he'd changed his views and banished racism from his discourse.

Malcolm's behaviour had been excessive throughout his life: first in his addictions, then in his marginalisation and, after prison, in his hatred of others because of their skin colour. It seems likely he experienced his lighter

```
Name: ♂ Malcolm X
born on Tu., 19 May 1925          Time:        10:25 p.m.
in Omaha, NE (US)                 Univ.Time:   4:25 20 May
95w56, 41n16                      Sid. Time:   13:50:31
Natal Chart (Method: Greene Anglo / Placidus)
```

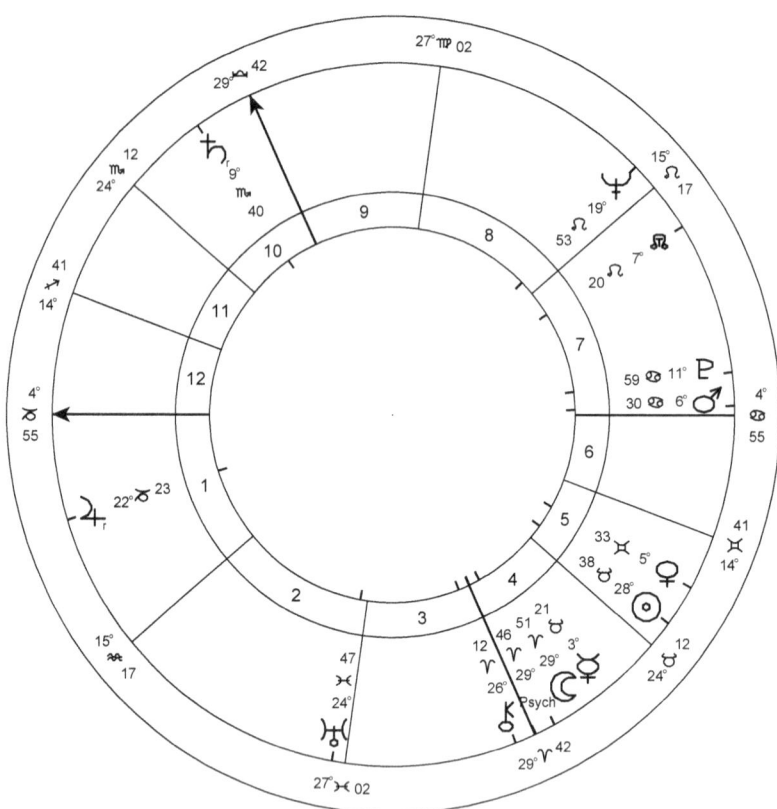

skin than his father and siblings as a betrayal of his "own" people. The way his mother treated him as the grandson of a white rapist conditioned him to hate Whites, the white man in him, and to do whatever it took to earn his place in his black family. The conjunction of the Moon and Psyche symbolises that the relationship with his mother was crucial to Malcolm's access to inner qualities necessary for a healthy expression of Venus. The revelation is an important part of the myth of Psyche: when Malcolm shone his oil lamp on his mother, he saw more than divine beauty. He saw Louise's hatred of a part of herself that he shared with her. As Malcolm set out in search of the beauty he saw, he also had to hate what his mother found ugly. The Moon here evokes themes of clan, origin, the past and its memory, and the body. What's more, because the Moon reflects the light of the Sun, Malcolm continued to construct his identity by seeing himself in the lunar mirror, where he wasn't black. In his autobiography, Malcolm X explained: "I learned to hate every drop of white rapist blood that is in me."[50] And so, in order to prove his 'black' origins, he spent his whole life in search of an identity as the saviour of African Americans. In Malcolm's chart, Psyche is exactly conjunct the IC, making the connection between self-discovery and his roots, his household, his origins and his ancestry: it was in the fourth house that his wisdom was to be revealed.

Finally, significant relationships (Psyche) were certainly a means of accessing his emotions and body throughout his life. However, we don't know whether his long-term relationship with his wife allowed him to get closer to his emotions, as little information is available about Malcolm X's personal life. Malcolm's Psyche is in Aries, conjunct the Moon as already mentioned, but also conjunct Chiron. His inner qualities may have something to do with healing and teaching, and with Aries involved, the feeling of being potent, of being able to change things, is crucial. Chiron, Psyche and the Moon all conjoin the IC, so the physical body serves as an outer expression of origin and belonging. His mother's wound (Moon-Chiron) is the mirror in which Malcolm should have seen his own beauty (Psyche), but his mother's hatred of her own skin colour made him a crusader. By assuming the role of "saviour" of African Americans, Malcolm X was probably able to express his Moon-Chiron conjunction creatively, thereby giving life to the qualities symbolised by Psyche in Aries in aspect to the Moon and Chiron. This enabled him to regain his sense of self-worth and value, and to achieve his solar immortality.

Diana Spencer

Diana Spencer had a quincunx between the Moon and Psyche, with an orb of 3°10. As seen earlier with Malcolm X, she first perceived the beauty of the Divine in her mother. Psyche in quincunx to the Moon is an invitation to look closely at the relationship with the mother, to find out whether it's helped the child to develop the qualities they need to build healthy and worthwhile emotional relationships. Diana's mother experienced a form of martyrdom that took Diana years to recognise: mistreated by her husband,

---

50 Alex Haley, *The Autobiography of Malcolm X as told to Alex Haley* (Turtleback Books 1987).

she wanted to leave him. But her own mother, Diana's grandmother, was opposed: by taking her children away from their father, her daughter was depriving them of the possibility of meeting a member of the royal family. So she testified against her in the divorce proceedings, saying her son-in-law was a good husband and father and her daughter was unstable. Diana's mother suffered abuse at the hands of her husband, then betrayal by her mother and the loss of custody of her children. It was of course an extraordinary thing in those days for a father to be granted full and sole custody of his children. They resented their mother terribly and it's likely they were victims of parental alienation, hearing only their father's side of the story. Diana's younger brother told *The Sunday Times* in 2020: "Our father was a quiet and constant source of love, but our mother wasn't cut out for maternity. Not her fault, she couldn't do it. She was in love with someone else – infatuated, really." Diana resented her for most of her life, saying she'd never have left her boys. Their relationship was very complicated, alternating between periods of seeing each other and whole years without a word, especially after the Princess's wedding. Her mother didn't come to the wedding because she couldn't stand the pressure, so Diana didn't speak to her for four years. At the end of her life, she used to return her mother's letters unopened because her mother had publicly insulted her for her choice of lovers, two of whom were Muslim. Diana's mother was a woman deeply wounded by the important relationships in her life: her husband, her mother and her children. She was unable to embody the divine beauty Diana was seeking. Because Diana had such high expectations of her mother, she left her with an image of everything she didn't want to be.

As previously said, relationship is the means by which the asteroid Psyche puts us in touch with a part of ourselves: when Psyche is in contact with the Moon, the relationship with the mother is crucial in revealing the inner qualities represented by the sign and house of Psyche. But when the mother is absent (as with Gérard de Nerval), or fails, or doesn't value herself at all, the quest is more difficult. And if she pushes the child away or doesn't see the beauty in them, the child may find it difficult to appropriate what belongs to them, lacking the mirror that would have reflected their inner beauty. Later on, there will certainly be a tendency to form other lunar-type relationships in order to reveal the qualities described by the asteroid and to be able to honour Venus afterwards.

Diana Spencer is best known for her marriage to King Charles III. She wanted the public to remember this relationship was tainted from the start by her husband's affair with Camilla Parker-Bowles. The reality of their marriage was much more complicated, as were the relationships in Diana's life. Reading the various biographies of her, it's hard to find a single week when she was single. The list of her lovers after the birth of her children is astonishing, especially that she often had several at the same time. Many men, such as John Fitzgerald Kennedy, may have behaved in the same way, but they were aware these liaisons were recreational. Diana, on the other hand, was desperate for love, or so she kept telling her friends. She was incredibly demanding about the proof of love she expected: she could call her lover several times a day to ask the same questions and be reassured that he loved her. Her behaviour was tyrannical, according to one of her lovers, with whom the relationship lasted more than three years. Transferred to Germany for two years by his military superiors, he was denied the right to see her from one day to the next because she considered his transfer a betrayal. He risked court martial if he refused, or at least the ruin of his career, but she wouldn't listen. She felt a permanent emptiness inside, one of the manifestations of which was her eating disorders.

For Diana, the feeling of abandonment by her mother certainly conditioned her later behaviour in love. The relationship that was supposed to enable her to appropriate her own Psyche failed her, and she subsequently sought new relationships of the lunar type, but within a loving framework. But no matter how many lovers she had, she was unable to access her inner self. As seen earlier, the Moon goddesses refuse to help Psyche, but Diana continued to expect her lovers to reassure her and give her the emotional security she needed. She had to leave this way of relating, but she needed help to do so. Diana received life-saving insights from two women with whom she was able to form lasting, lunar-like relationships and who helped her to regain her sense of self-worth: her astrologer and her psychiatrist. It was they who enabled her to find a humanitarian calling and to use her gift to bring joy and relief to suffering people. Diana's generosity of heart was particularly evident in her last decade, thanks to the guidance of her astrologer, who saw in her a very "spiritual" person. Her eating problems were also treated by an acupuncturist. It was then that she was able to establish a healthy, lunar relationship with her stepmother, her father's second wife, whom she'd rejected all her life. She even declared

152   *In The Name of Love – The Asteroid Psyche*

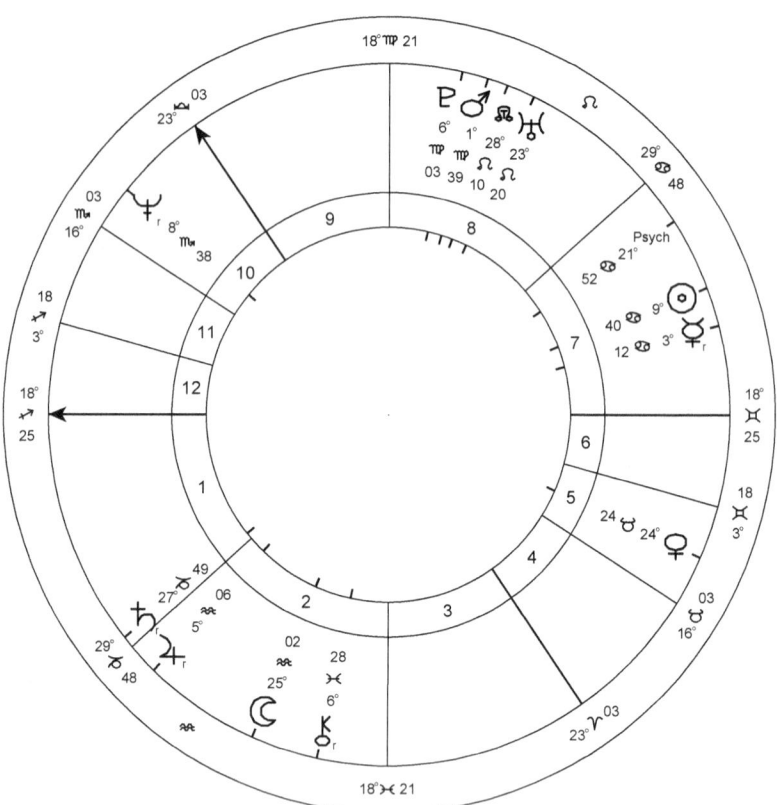

```
Name: ♀ Diana Spencer
born on Sa., 1 July 1961        Time:        7:45 p.m.
in Sandringham, ENG (UK)        Univ.Time: 18:45
0e30, 52n50                     Sid. Time: 13:25:18
Natal Chart (Method: Greene Anglo / Placidus)
```

she was more of a mother to her than her own. Her stepmother's Pluto at 19°17 Cancer was conjunct her Psyche, and this relationship therefore triggered Diana's Psyche, providing her with a surrogate Cupid. After a desperate search for emotional stability in her relationships and the means to make Psyche her own, it was finally relationships with three women that allowed Diana to move forward. She was finally able to truly live her Venus.

In the Princess's chart, Psyche is in Cancer and in the seventh house. The qualities of Cancer, its ability to care for the vulnerable – in Diana's case, her inner child – had to be revealed for her to form meaningful Venusian relationships. This was also the sign in which her Sun was: the Moon, as ruler of the Sun and Psyche, and in aspect to the asteroid, had a major role to play in the expression of her individuality, in the meaning she gave to her existence. At the end of her life she was able to radiate natural empathy and the ability to bring joy and comfort to the most vulnerable, and this became her life's vocation. As Psyche was in aspect to the Moon, she needed lunar relationships, with her psychiatrist, her astrologer and then her mother-in-law, to reveal the qualities of Cancer, those specifically necessary for the healthy expression of Venus: listening to her inner self and taking into account the wounds of her childhood and her relationship with her parents. Her Venus in Taurus ultimately sought simple love relationships in the shared pleasure of being together and in a presumed sensuality. Once Psyche's qualities in Cancer were revealed, she was better able to choose her companions according to her values and not according to their ability to give her the security she'd lacked as a child. She was also able to form "just" partnerships in which each person played their own role without continuing to demand that the other play the role of surrogate parent.

Émilie

One of my clients, Émilie, who had a Moon-Psyche conjunction with an orb of 2°04, had a similar struggle with her mother. She was the oldest of five children, the second child being a boy two years her junior. Her mother always showed a clear preference for her brother, whom she saw as gifted in everything: mathematics, music and sports. To Émilie's mother, her daughter was less gifted, so she was never encouraged. Émilie reacted by doing everything she could to please her mother: taking an interest in her passions, adopting her style of dress and choosing the same studies as her. This desperate race suggests this woman had seen divine beauty in her mother from birth. She needed a fruitful relationship to find the beauty within herself. But her mother, on learning her daughter wanted to study medicine like her, told her she couldn't succeed, and Émilie failed and eventually gave up trying to earn her mother's respect and esteem. Like Malcolm X, she felt less loved than the other siblings, left out, and the lunar mirror reflected back to her a negative image of herself, unable to satisfy her mother. Émilie suffered from eating disorders, various psychosomatic problems and changed careers four times because she couldn't find her way. It's clear this was a lunar problem (the body, the emotions) coupled with a problem of access to the self.

Like Diana, she was later able to access her emotions through therapeutic relationships: her psychologist on the one hand, but also a relationship within her religious community, a woman who acted as a counsellor and guide, enabling her to accept and then calm her emotional feelings. Having been able to contemplate divine beauty in the context of a lunar relationship, she was able to try to make it her own. In her chart, Psyche is in Virgo and in the fifth house: discernment was therefore an essential value for her. She decided to put as much distance as possible between herself and her mother, seeing her only twice a year. With Virgo's wisdom, she sorted out her values, needs and desires, and entered into a relationship with the future father of her children. She also learnt a craft at which she proved very talented and which enabled her to make a living. Emilie had to wait until the first return of Saturn to stop trying to be like her mother. It was only by opposing her mother, by having the courage not to be like her, and by standing up to her when she was forced to do so, that Émilie was able to reveal the qualities of her Psyche in Virgo.

Robert Schumann

In Robert Schumann's chart, Psyche is trine the Moon, with an orb of 0°58. He was born to a mother who was an amateur musician and a father who was a bookseller and translator. While his father was still alive, he saw his son's talent for music: he even asked Carl Maria von Weber to take care of his son, but was refused. His father died when Robert was sixteen and his widowed mother preferred to envisage a more stable career for her son. In 1828 she enrolled him at the University of Leipzig, where he soon became bored and isolated from the other students. By this time, he was already experiencing a great sadness that could be interpreted as depression. After two years, he finally left law and became a student of his future wife's father, the pianist Friedrich Wieck. He informed his mother of this resolution, who replied with a letter warning him of the risks of such a decision, which had no effect.

Throughout his life, Schumann was plagued by various illnesses, culminating in his famous attempt to drown himself in the Rhine and his admission to an asylum, where he died two years later. When he began his piano studies in Wieck's house, he wrote letters to his mother complaining of many pains: in his stomach, head and heart. He had an exaggerated fear of illness, with various symptoms that lasted a few weeks and then disappeared as suddenly as they had appeared. As a pianist of European stature, his wife Clara Schumann made several concert tours to Russia. During an 1844 concert tour, he reported anxiety, phobias, sleep disorders, great fatigue, abulia and crying fits. He even mentioned trembling limbs. He underwent two water cures which had no effect on his problems. Ear pain and tinnitus also gradually appeared. From 1850 he complained of anxiety attacks and dizziness. He suffered from insomnia and moments of distraction when he was unaware of what was happening. His speech became increasingly slurred. His problems came to a head when he began to suffer from auditory hallucinations and physical pain which, according to his wife, made him "scream".[51] Shortly afterwards, he attempted to drown himself.

Schumann inherited his musical talents as well as his health problems from his mother. We know Johanna Schumann was prone to anxiety attacks and went through periods of depression, sadness and asthenia. In her correspondence she described these attacks, during which she had no taste for anything and felt incapable of intellectual effort. Playing the harpsichord and writing poetry, she clearly had the same sensitive and artistic nature as her last son. The trine between Schumann's Moon and the asteroid Psyche indicates that he needed to admire certain qualities in his mother, like Psyche, who, contemplating her husband's beauty, falls in love with him and, thanks to that love, finds the energy to develop her inner qualities. As they grow up, children with a Moon-Psyche aspect realise what they saw in their mother doesn't belong to them, although at first, because they weren't clearly separated from their mother, they couldn't believe it. Each stage of separation between mother and child (and the Saturn cycle comes to mind) is a moment when the child is robbed of their Cupid, when they can therefore find the energy they need to do their own labours. In Schumann's case, Venus is in Cancer conjunct the descendant, in the seventh house. A man of his time with such a natal position was at risk of projecting his Venus onto his partner, making her embody the very feminine qualities of a Venus in Cancer. But Schumann's artistic vocation demanded that he embody this Venus himself, at least through his art. The gift of Psyche in

---

51 Clara and Robert Schumann, *The Diary of Robert and Clara Schumann* (Koehler und Amelang, 1934).

Taurus is the tenacity of the sign, enabling Schumann to have the courage to make choices based on his values, and to stand by those choices over time. She is also trine the Moon, so the wisdom of Taurus must also be coloured by that of the Moon, which means listening to the inner self and child is necessary to build meaningful relationships. As Schumann's first Cupid was his mother, he unconsciously identified with her because she embodied the eminently desirable beauty of the divine. This identification may have led to the sharing of disabling physical or emotional symptoms. Although Johanna didn't encourage him to become a musician, with the laudable aim of securing him a more stable life as a lawyer, she loved him dearly and called him *lichter punkt*, point of light. This made it easier for Schumann to claim Psyche as his own, for his mother implicitly acknowledged his right to identify with what was desirable and beautiful in her.

Maria Montessori

Maria Montessori has already been mentioned in the chapter on the encounter between the progressed Sun and Psyche. In her birth chart, Montessori had a quincunx between the Moon and Psyche, with an orb of 0°33. It would be an understatement to say she too was greatly influenced by her mother and the relationship she developed with her. Renilde Stoppani was incredibly well-educated by the standards of her time in Italy: she read a lot, and for a woman to be able to write her name was a source of great pride. Montessori also showed a natural aptitude for academia very quickly, and she was able to pass the exam required to enter medical school. But her father, who knew such a choice would be incompatible with family life, opposed her vocation. Her mother, on the other hand, encouraged her and helped her pay for her studies.

According to Maria's son, Mario, the relationship was idyllic: "They had a real adoration for each other. Their bond was stronger than the love that usually unites mother and daughter." But there was a downside. According to a descendant, Carolina Montessori, Renilde lived her life by proxy, through her daughter's success: "I think her mother had transferred all her ambitions to her daughter."[52] The episode of Maria's unwanted pregnancy speaks volumes: while she was stunned and unable to make a decision,

---

52 Maria Montessori, *Maria Montessori Sails to America*, translated and introduced by Carolina Montessori (Montessori-Pierson Publishing Company, 2013).

it was her mother who took matters into her own hands. According to Carolina, she told her: "You have done what no woman has ever done in Italy: you are a scientist, a doctor, you are everything, and now you are going to lose everything for a child". She saved Montessori's career, of course. But you can't help feeling a little uneasy when you see the influence this mother had on her adult daughter, and when you realise how much Maria seems to have lived according to her mother's wishes. From the moment she was born, Maria saw divine beauty in her mother, fell in love with it and wanted to make it her own. The ground was all the more fertile for deep identification because her mother seemed to want her daughter to fulfil the destiny she didn't. In Maria's case, Psyche is in Gemini and in the tenth house: the position in this house strengthens the symbolic link with the mother, and it also points to the importance of vocation in revealing the qualities symbolised by the asteroid. Maria was able to demonstrate the qualities of this air sign in the development of her method: far from the dogmas of the time which she was supposed to follow, she used the qualities of adaptability of the sign to learn from the children themselves. She accumulated knowledge and experience through encounters and in the field, not according to any particular theory. Maria needed the relationship with her mother to find this beauty in herself, and it seems her mother helped her to do so, even if the aspect in play, the quincunx, could evoke something more ambivalent.

Louis XIV, King of France

In the Sun King's chart, the Moon in Leo squares Psyche in Scorpio, with an orb of 2°33. It's no exaggeration to say the King's mother, Anne of Austria, was of great importance in her son's life. It was certainly the most important relationship in his life. The only other person who could claim to have had such an influence on the great king was his second wife, Madame de Maintenon. Louis XIII, his father, died when Louis was four and a half years old, and Anne of Austria took over the regency. She was assisted by the Italian born Cardinal Mazarin, but the two of them faced many problems, the most important of which was the revolt of the princes, the Fronde. Louis saw how his mother behaved during the darkest hours of her life. He admired her courage, her fighting spirit, her cunning and her intelligence.

In the Sun King's chart, the Moon is conjunct Venus in Leo. The luminary and the planet both square Psyche, so the beauty he saw in his mother was also Venusian. Louis inherited from Anne a very strong taste for parties and the *belle galanterie* of women's society. As an adult, he frequented the Queen Mother's salon. His mistresses played a real role in his life, for he wasn't content with their beauty; he wanted them to be intelligent and cultured, and he enjoyed their company. Saturn, in early Aquarius, completes a T-square with Psyche in Scorpio and the Moon-Venus conjunction in Leo. The mother-son relationship was marked by affection and respect, but also by a necessary distance, given the times and the status of Anne of Austria, regent of the kingdom. She was constantly preoccupied with matters of state and remained so until her son came of age. She was also aware of her rank and birth, having been educated at the very rigid Spanish court. Saturn is therefore also part of what he admired in his mother and then tried to make his own, as it's linked to the Moon and Psyche. Finally, Pluto completes this particularly complex maternal image, being quincunx Psyche, and sextile the Moon. As a child, Louis knew very well who was in power over him, even though he was educated by a governess, then a governor and a tutor. An anecdote illustrates this perfectly: in May 1647, during a trip to Picardy, Louis had a disagreement with his mother. He said, "That's the way I want it." The Queen replied: "I will show you that you have no power and that I do. It's been too long since you've been whipped." After bursting into tears, the sovereign threw himself on his mother's knees and said: "Mother, I beg you to forgive me; I promise never to have any will but yours."[53] Having reached the age of royal majority, set at thirteen, Louis XIV was invested with royal powers by his mother. However, as he didn't yet seem able to do without her, he asked her to remain the head of his council. He waited until Mazarin's death, ten years later, to dismiss his mother and rule alone.

The natal square between the Moon and Psyche shows that Louis's first Cupid would be his mother: their relationship and his longing for her divine beauty would provide the fuel for his inner quest. But the square suggests his mother would have a more ambiguous attitude towards her son than Robert Schumann's mother. She would probably not have called him a point of light, as her Spanish upbringing wouldn't have allowed her

---

53 Thierry Sarmant, *Homme et roi* (Tallandier 2014).

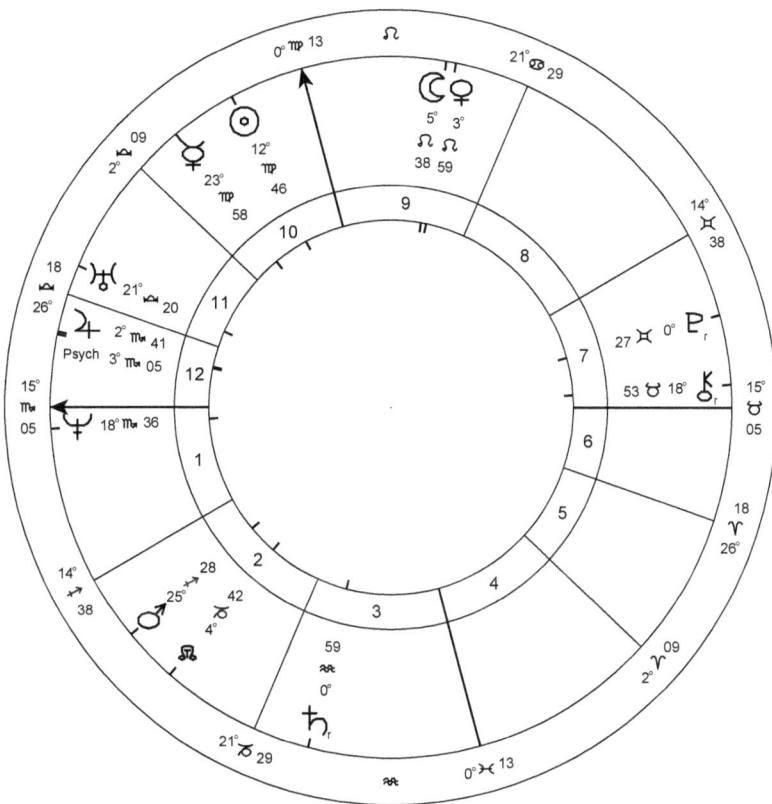

to do so: it would have been a sign of weakness to show such affection towards her son. Nevertheless, she took much better care of her two boys than most other royal mothers. The Sun King's Moon in Leo also evokes the golden child, the favourite on whom the mother's expectations rest. But she knew what awaited Louis, and so did her utmost to instil in him a sense of duty, of his rank, but not of his personal worth. A king's duty is to his country and his God, not to himself or his personal happiness. Louis's attempt to appropriate the beauty he saw in his mother may therefore have met with a lukewarm reception. From his point of view, the qualities of Scorpio, the sign of Psyche, had probably belonged to his mother for many years. It's true that his mother fully embodied them in the way she exercised power, with Pluto right on her midheaven.

Louis XIV modelled himself on his mother: his sense of duty, his piety, his authority and his distance from his subjects were inspired by those of Anne of Austria. She was for him a mother, a father and an exemplary monarch, as evidenced by a line quoted at her death: "More than a great Queen, she was a great King."[54] In the King's chart, Psyche is conjunct Jupiter in the twelfth house. This placement suggests an ancestral heritage, recalling the line of Spanish monarchs from which Anne of Austria descended, and the sign of Scorpio in this context refers to a certain secret exercise of power. The conjunction to Jupiter indicates this planet is essential in the process of unveiling Scorpio's inner beauty, and as Jupiter is the King of the Gods, the symbolism of the exercise of power is recalled. In other words, the way Anne wielded power held an irresistible attraction for Louis, and he was able to discover the same beauty within himself once his mother was removed from power and relations with her had become distant. His self-esteem was undoubtedly linked to his influence (Venus in Leo), but this was only possible because of the way he exercised power: the Scorpio qualities he seems to have inherited from his ancestors were therefore crucial.

---

54 Claude Dulong, *Anne d'Autriche* (Hachette, 2000).

Some thoughts on Moon-Psyche aspects

As seen earlier, in early early childhood, a child with a Moon-Psyche aspect needs to admire something beautiful and unique in their mother in order to engage the psychic energy needed to find his own inner beauty, which is reflected by the asteroid. The mother's personality, and the way in which it interacts with that of her child, is therefore crucial. The child may develop the qualities of the sign of their Psyche by following the path of their mother, like Louis XIV, Schumann or Maria Montessori, or, on the contrary, they may find their mother's model repulsive, which urges them to take back what belongs to them. In both cases, it's the relationship with the mother that provides the starting point for the quest.

In this last section, I propose some elements for reflection on the asteroid and her meaning, which aren't based on biographical elements. Let's take the example of Moon-Jupiter aspects: they can symbolise an emotional nature that needs to experience exalted states, with a taste for adventure or a certain theatricality. They can also mean (especially the square, the opposition or the conjunction) that the mother had these qualities but was unable to live them out because of a personal situation in which she found herself trapped. She may also have been unable to find a creative solution to a dilemma between the need for security, family responsibilities and a *puella* spirit, an eternal young girl who wants to live intensely. The Moon-Psyche aspects, in addition to what has already been mentioned, could be interpreted in the same way: the mother was unable to rise to the challenge of carrying out her Venusian labours. Lost in a family life, with little room to honour Venus, she lost her sense of personal worth by giving a central place to lunar values. She would then be unable to reveal the inner beauty symbolised by Psyche, and the conflict would be passed on to her child. The child must then find their own answers to make the relationship a driving force for personal fulfilment, without being trapped by lunar issues of emotional security and material comfort. We don't have the charts of the mothers of the people mentioned in this chapter, with the exception of Anne of Austria. Interestingly, she also had Psyche in the twelfth house, as did her son, but especially conjunct the ascendant. This means Psyche was destined to serve as her psychic guide: if, for lack of choice, she, as the daughter of a king and then queen of France, was unable to give Psyche the importance it should have had, her son inherited the mission of giving life to a function that hadn't found its place in the maternal psyche.

The Fathers and Mothers of Psychoanalysis – Psyche and Jupiter, Saturn, and Pluto

The links between the field of psychoanalysis and the myth of Psyche are numerous and striking: unveiling is central, as the analyst seeks to make conscious what is not. Symbolic immortality has to do with wholeness: whether in myth or in psychoanalysis, the aim is to rediscover a buried or lost part of oneself; Psyche rediscovers her Cupid and her own divine beauty, and the analysand rediscovers what has been banished from their consciousness and prevented them from becoming what they were meant to be. Ultimately, this self-knowledge is achieved through the other, and the listening of the analyst is essential to this process.

In the charts of those psychoanalysts who have done most to enrich the debates around Freud's "discovery" and to advance psychoanalytic practice and theory, the two planets we find so frequently in relation to Psyche that it can't be left to chance are Saturn and Pluto. Let's start with Freud, whose chart shows a close conjunction between Psyche and Saturn with an orb of 1°32. For Marie-Louise von Franz, it's a very close trine, 0°06, with Psyche on the North Node. For Françoise Dolto it's a trine with an orb of 1°37. Sandor Ferenczi has a 2°13 square in his chart. Wilhem Reich also has a 1°46 square, and Josef Breuer has a trine with an orb of 0°40. Finally, Donald Winnicott has a quincunx with an orb of 0°46.

For others, it's Pluto: Melanie Klein's chart shows an exact conjunction (0°01) between Psyche and Pluto. Emma Jung has a square with an orb of 0°03. Karl Abraham's chart also displays a square, with an orb of 3°25. For René Spitz and Anna Freud, the orb is wider: a 7° orb square for the former and an 8°06 orb conjunction for the latter. However, this square and conjunction are all the more important because the asteroid Psyche is particularly significant in their charts: Spitz's chart shows an almost exact quincunx between the Sun and Psyche, while the asteroid conjoins the ascendant in Anna Freud's chart.

Finally, some famous analysts had aspects between Psyche and both Saturn and Pluto: Carl Jung, Otto Rank and Jacques Lacan, leader of a famous French school of psychoanalysis. For Lacan, there is a 2°48 conjunction to Pluto and a 2°44 quincunx to Saturn. In Rank's case, Psyche is trine Pluto (3°29) and Saturn (4°47). Jung's case is the most significant: the asteroid Psyche is conjunct Pluto (1°00), square Saturn (0°41) and also quincunx Jupiter (0°43), as we shall see later.

Why do we find aspects between the asteroid Psyche and Saturn and/or Pluto in the charts of the greatest men and women of psychoanalysis? Both planets are associated with inner riches that need to be revealed, with Saturn being the gold of the ancient astrologers and Pluto, the god of the Underworld, ruling over subterranean riches. Saturn, the last of the visible planets for the ancients, was the limit of the visible. It was therefore associated with occupations that made the invisible visible. The word Pluto comes from the Greek Πλοῦτος, meaning wealth or abundance. Pluto-Psyche aspects mean that the process of revealing inner wisdom through a relationship involves the planet Pluto and his symbolism. Pluto-Psyche aspects also mean that the qualities of Psyche are coloured by Pluto, by the wisdom inherent in this planet. The qualities symbolised by the asteroid in the birth chart have the peculiarity of being both necessary for the establishment of healthy emotional relationships, and of being unveiled, revealed, by a relationship. People with a major aspect between Psyche and Pluto therefore need to be in touch with certain aspects of the Underworld in order to honour Venus; and the relationships at stake when Psyche is activated by transit or progression will also activate Pluto, which means these people need to delve deeper to find out why the relationship may have caused them suffering or how they went wrong in it. Since they can't escape this dive into the depths, this visit to Proserpine's realm, people with a Psyche-Pluto aspect will then use their subtle and clear vision of what's at stake in relationships as soon as they become emotionally involved. From then on they may develop a keen interest in what's unconscious, what's projected onto the other person, and in identifying limiting and invisible conditioning. These people can use the potential of the connection (Psyche) made between two unconscious minds (Pluto), that of the analyst and of the patient, to reveal what is hidden and repressed (unconscious qualities symbolised by Psyche). The term "depth psychology" used to describe

Jung's work perfectly illustrates the close conjunction between Pluto and Psyche in his birth chart.

As far as Saturn is concerned, the connection with psychoanalysis deserves a closer look. Hesiod's *Theogony* is worth considering: in this, Cronus puts an end to the first reign, that of Ouranos and his mother Gaia, by taking the risk of castrating his father. Answering the call of his mother, who could no longer bear the thought of her lover preventing her children from being born, he was the only one of the twelve Titans to take the scythe offered by Gaia. The youngest of his siblings, he dares to confront his father and, when Ouranos is defeated, finds himself king in his place, but alone: here he is, a symbolic orphan, forced to assume a role for which he has not been trained. Just as Chiron, the orphan rejected by his mother and abandoned by his father, can symbolise in our chart the ability to take care of others in the manner of an adoptive father, so Saturn-Cronus, who wasn't supported in his function as chief of the gods can symbolise in our chart the ability to guide, to serve as a mentor to others, or even as a teacher.

Cronus, once king, fears above all that he himself will be replaced by his children, and denies them the right to live by devouring them. This symbolic denial of what is becoming, this fear of what is not under control, can be found in our natal chart, where Saturn is. The planet represents the places where we're prey to doubt, where we don't feel legitimate, where we can take a defensive stance, for example, by doing everything in our power to become experts on the subject. In this way, Saturn in aspect to Psyche can give rise to a fear of relationships and what they can reveal about us, a feeling we've been unfairly deprived of something we admired in someone else, a difficulty in developing the qualities of Psyche necessary for Venus expression. With the planet Saturn we must always work hard to overcome this feeling of imperfection and inadequacy. The expertise we gain from this can then be invested in a therapeutic context, to help others find ways of revealing the qualities that need to be expressed in order to build meaningful and fulfilling relationships. The planet Saturn in contact with Psyche also evokes the need to establish clear boundaries between oneself and others, to develop autonomy in relationships. This skill is indispensable for a psychoanalyst, and it also enables them to avoid confusion and excessive empathy when listening to the client (remember that Psyche must not show misplaced empathy in her fourth labour). The analysts mentioned above, whose Psyche is in close aspect to Saturn, were all teachers. They were founders of psychoanalytic schools, or at least leaders of schools of thought. Thus, in the charts of Freud, Jung, von Franz, Lacan, Dolto, Winnicott and Ferenczi, Saturn-Psyche symbolises the tutor, the one on whom the analysand can rely in order to achieve completeness and self-knowledge, but also the teacher, the one who passes on their theories or creates a "school". Finally, they are the expert, the one who works tirelessly to perfect their knowledge of the human psyche and to find how to reveal what's unconscious.

Finally, let's mention the aspects between Jupiter and Psyche, which are also common among psychoanalysts: Freud (square, 3°33) Jung (quincunx, 0°43), Emma Jung (square, 2°23), Klein (square, 2°31) von Franz (conjunction, 4°38), Dolto (square, 4°31), Ferenczi (sextile, 2°46), Reich (conjunction, 3°02), Breuer (trine, 0°31) Adler (sextile, 3°14), Spitz (sextile 3°57), Laforgue (trine, 0°55). In Greek mythology, Jupiter embodies the father who supports his children, in contrast to Cronus, who devours them. At Artemis's request, he gives her the right to own a bow and arrow like her brother – in other words, the right to pursue her goals. With Psyche-Jupiter contacts, the issues raised in a relationship by transits and progressions triggering Psyche also bring Jupiter into play, and Jupiter is necessary for an authentic expression of the planet Venus. The issues of self-confidence, optimism about life and personal expansion need to be challenged when these people enter into important relationships. They have already experienced the extent to which a relationship can teach them to contact this Jupiterian enthusiasm, as long as it encourages access to themselves, self-reflection and the unveiling of their qualities. They may therefore wish to give others the same opportunities, knowing they aren't innate but have to be acquired through experience. These people can then be found in a supportive therapeutic role, embodying Jupiter for those who need it. This tendency applies to any kind of helping and supporting relationship, or even to teaching, for example.

Psyche in Cross-Aspects: Thoughts on Synastry

Psychoanalysts

The field of psychoanalysis will again serve as our field of investigation for the influence of Psyche in synastry. I will then focus on the British royal family, which is of immense interest in that it has members whose time of birth and many biographical details are known. Finally, the synastry between the men of the Kennedy family will be studied.

Let's start with the most famous duo in the world of psychoanalysis: Sigmund Freud and Carl Gustav Jung. At first, Freud thought he'd found in Jung a disciple and an interlocutor who would enable him to develop his thinking and make it more fruitful. However, the differences between the two men were so great that they led to a rupture that proved equally painful for both. For Jung, Psyche at 24°31 Taurus is at the midpoint of Freud's Mercury-Uranus conjunction. So Freud served as Cupid for Jung, at least in the beginning: there's no doubt that the genius of Freud allowed Jung to progress in his self-discovery – it served as a support point for him to develop the qualities of his Psyche conjunct Pluto in Taurus. And in doing the work necessary to develop this aspect of his talent, Jung in turn stimulated the fertility of the Master's natal conjunction and allowed the starry Uranian heavens to re-seed his Mercurian thought. In Freud's case, Psyche trines Jung's Saturn: the former at 26°01 of Gemini, the latter at 24°12 of Aquarius. Freud therefore saw in Jung a Saturnian beauty that could serve as a guide in his quest. As Freud's Psyche was closely conjunct Saturn in his natal chart, he was surely more sensitive to the righteousness he perceived in Jung, his independence of thought and his ability to see things from above.

Another collaboration, this time between two women, allows us to move forward in the study of Psyche in synastry: that between Emma Jung and Marie-Louise von Franz. Emma Jung worked for many years on the

Grail myth and left her work unfinished when she died. It was von Franz who completed her book at her request. In both women's charts, Psyche is particularly important: in Jung's chat it's conjunct the Moon, and in von Franz's it's conjunct the North Node. The Psyche cross-aspects between their two birth charts seem to leave nothing to chance: their Psyches are exactly square (0°03), and Jung's Psyche is exactly sextile von Franz's Saturn (0°02), while von Franz's Psyche is almost exactly square Jung's Pluto (0°07). As said earlier, Psyche-Saturn and/or Psyche-Pluto aspects are extremely common among the founders of psychoanalysis. Saturn and Pluto therefore seem to be the planets which, in psychoanalysis, most effectively serve the revelatory potential of the relationship (Psyche). The two women were each other's Cupids, one urging the other to develop her Psyche through either Saturn's beauty or Pluto's. The Jungian von Franz's chart also shows an interesting synastry with Carl Jung's chart: their Psyches are also square (3°08), and von Franz's Psyche is therefore conjunct Carl Jung's Saturn (3°27).

Another long-distance collaboration of interest in the study of Psyche in synastry is that between Anna Freud and Sandor Ferenczi. Ferenczi worked on the theme of identification with the aggressor, and his chart shows a close conjunction between Mars and Psyche, at 3°24 and 2°42 of Scorpio, respectively. Since Psyche is revealed through relationships, her conjunction to Mars in Ferenczi's chart may be at the root of his interest in identifying with the aggressor. Indeed, with Psyche in a sign ruled by and in conjunction to Mars, Ferenczi may have tended to choose as his Cupid people with a marked assertiveness, or possibly aggressors, at least in the symbolic sense of the term. Anna Freud later took up the concept introduced by Ferenczi and published *The Ego and the Mechanisms of Defence*. In Anna Freud's chart, Psyche is at 3°40 of Gemini, in a very close quincunx to Ferenczi's Psyche-Mars conjunction. What's more, in her case Mars is in opposition to Psyche, although the orb is wide (just under 10°), and it also conjoins the descendant. These peculiarities may explain why Ferenczi's work attracted the attention of Anna Freud, and highlights that contacts between Mars and Psyche may arouse a particular interest in the aggressor-victim relationship and the role of early aggression in the construction of the psyche.

The British Royal Family

To study the more emotional effects of Psyche in synastry, the British royal family is ideal. It's rare to have both biographical information and birth data for several members of the same family. The heirs to the royal crown who knew Queen Elizabeth II before her death all have an aspect between their natal Psyches and her Pluto. The latter is in quincunx to Charles's, in sextile to William's, and in trine to George's. These aspects underline the role that Elizabeth II's power played in her relationship with her son, grandson and great-grandson. While we know she prepared Charles and then William for their future role as king, this is probably not the case with George, who was only nine when she died. But the relationship between Elizabeth II and her three heirs was, at least in part, Plutonian, marked by the seal of fate and the exercise of power. Pluto is the planet that symbolises what must be and what we don't choose – fate. We first encounter it at birth, when our genetic heritage is imposed on us and becomes part of our destiny that we can't choose, like our family environment. If you're the first-born child of a royal family, Pluto enters the family relationships and reveals to the heir who they are, the future king or queen. The three heirs to the throne perceived in Elizabeth II a Plutonian beauty that was necessary for them to access a part of themselves. The way in which she embodied power awakened in them an inner quest that was all the more necessary as they'd one day be called upon to assume that power. For them, the Queen was a Plutonian Cupid. The power and sense of destiny embodied by the Queen were therefore transformative elements for Charles, William and George, allowing them to reveal the qualities – as reflected by Psyche – they needed in order to have a sufficient sense of personal worth to feel they could fulfil their duty and destiny. It also influenced the ways in which they were able to use the characteristics of their Psyches in the emotional relationships they had or would have.

If we now look at relationships that are known to have been supportive, where the people involved have repeatedly stated what they owe the other, we find Jupiter and the Sun aspecting Psyche. For example, William had previously declared what he owed his grandfather Philip: "I feel lucky to have not just had his example to guide me, but his enduring presence well into my own adult life – both through good times and the hardest days. I will always be grateful that my wife had so many years to get to know my grandfather and for the kindness he showed her."[55] The role of his grandfather in his life is all the more important as we know his relationship with his own father, Charles, was much more complex, especially after Diana's death. William's and Philip's Psyches are sextile, and William's Psyche is conjunct Philip's Jupiter. Here we find the role of the good, supportive surrogate father, helping the child to become themself (Psyche), echoing what William said. Another person known to have been an unfailing supporter of William is his mother, Diana Spencer. The relationship wasn't without its ambiguities, as it seems Diana may have used her son as a confidante, but it's certain she loved him unconditionally. She was always immensely proud of him and his brother, and sometimes only found the strength to go on living because of them. William's Psyche is sextile his mother's Sun and her Neptune. He probably admired her very much. Diana, simply by being herself (the Sun), by radiating her light, was a mother who allowed her son to discover his wisdom, the qualities he needed to honour Venus (Psyche). William's Psyche is also opposite Diana's Chiron, which may reflect his sensitivity to his mother's suffering and/or the fact that his mother hurt him by exposing her to him. Diana's unfailing support (Sun) helped her son to develop the qualities of Virgo, the sign in which Psyche is found in William's birth chart. But he may also have needed Virgo's discerning wisdom in order not to feel invaded by his mother's wounds (Chiron and Neptune). His brother Harry also described his mother as very supportive, and as the youngest, he was fortunate not to be her confidante. There's a very close conjunction between Harry's Psyche and Diana's Jupiter (0°27), confirming that Psyche-Jupiter cross-aspects can reflect the fact that one of the individuals takes on the role of supportive parent, triggering self-fulfilment.

For their father Charles, the current British King, the supportive parent was his grandmother, the Queen Mother. There's a close trine (0°33) between Charles's Psyche and his grandmother's Sun. The Sun, which we've already seen in the cross-aspects between Diana and William, seems to provide support in one direction and great admiration in the other. After his grandmother's death, Charles said: "For me she meant everything and I had dreaded this moment along with, I know, countless

---

55 Prince William, *Statement by Prince William on the death of his grandfather, Prince Philip* (Kensington Palace / Royal Family, 12 April 2021).

others. [...] And oh how I shall miss those laughs and wonderful wisdom, born of so much experience and an innate sensitivity to life. She seemed gloriously unstoppable and ever since I was a child I adored her."[56] The warmth of the Sun gave him the energy he needed to find himself. On the other hand, he had a difficult relationship with his father, Philip. In the book *Diana: Story of a Princess*, published in 2001, author Tim Clayton quotes Penny Junor, a journalist specialising in the royal family, as saying, "Although he undoubtedly has great affection for Prince Charles, he has spent a lifetime criticizing him and quietly undermining his self-esteem."[57] Charles himself, through his authorised biography by Jonathan Dimbleby, portrayed his father in 1994 as harsh and domineering, making him cry on several occasions.[58] Charles's and Philip's Psyches are in quincunx, which is perhaps significant in itself. Most importantly, Charles's Psyche is in square to his father's Uranus, Jupiter and Saturn, which seems to confirm the image Charles had of his father: a cold, distant father who struggled to support his child and whose methods were based on discipline. Nevertheless, Charles's Psyche was trine Philip's Neptune, suggesting the relationship wasn't devoid of elements of admiration, which also helped to reveal the qualities reflected by Charles's Psyche.

Finally, while William, the heir to the throne, has always felt supported by his mother, he has a much more complex relationship with his father. While Harry, who wasn't yet in rebellion, had agreed on several occasions to declare in documentaries in 2017 and 2018 that Charles had been a good father, William reportedly refused to do the same. He felt manipulated on several occasions by his father, who was trying to make his relationship with Camilla acceptable. For a long time, he blamed him for Diana's death and for being absent after her death. Finally, those close to the Prince have stated that William regards his father-in-law, Michael Middleton, as a surrogate father. The rapprochement between father and son was made in the name of duty and because Queen Elizabeth II wanted it. But Charles wasn't experienced by William as a supportive father. Like Charles and

---

56 The Prince of Wales, *A Tribute by HRH The Prince of Wales following the death of Her Late Majesty Queen Elizabeth, The Queen Mother* (Clarence House / The Royal Family, London 30 March 2002).
57 Tim Clayton and Philip Craig, *Diana : Story of a Princess* (Simon & Schuster, 2001).
58 Jonathan Dimbleby, *The Prince of Wales: A Biography* (Little, Brown, 1994).

Philip, their Psyches are in a difficult cross-aspect: it's a tight square (0°11 orb). The other significant aspect is a conjunction between William's Psyche and Charles's Saturn (6°), an aspect which reflects William's sense of having had a father who could have embodied Saturnian beauty, but who seems to have shown his son only the cold and emotionally absent aspect of it.

The Kennedys

Another family, a royal family, or almost, allows us to study cross-aspects involving Psyche: the Kennedys. The thirty-fifth President of the United States of America, John Fitzgerald Kennedy, was the second son of Joseph Patrick Kennedy, known as Joe Senior, a brilliant and extremely wealthy businessman and ambassador. It wasn't JFK who was supposed to "reign", but his oldest brother, Joe Junior. Their father had had many children with his wife Rose, five girls and four boys, but his hopes rested on his two oldest. With less than two years between them, they were pitted against each other at an early age, first for sports, then for their studies (both went to Harvard) and for girls. The father adored his sons and wanted them to be happy, but he also had very clear expectations of them. One of them, the eldest, was to become President of the USA. But he also expected them to be good athletes, good students and to serve their country with honour. Pitting them against each other was a form of emulation for him, and he didn't realise how hard it was for John to bear. Suffering from what is now thought to be a serious autoimmune disease, he was constantly sick, and by the time he was a teenager he was suffering from back pain and colitis. He still had to live up to an older brother who was a good student, athletic and terribly handsome. From an early age, John learned to grit his teeth and hide his pain in order to follow in his older brother's footsteps and please his father. But tragedy struck to change the fates of John and Robert Kennedy: Joe Jr, who'd volunteered for an extremely risky mission, died in August 1944 when the plane he was flying for his country exploded over England. The fraternal struggle, which often seemed unequal to John, was finally lost: he confided to a very close friend, Lem Billings, that since his death, Joe Jr's superiority has been sealed in his father's heart.

Let's finish this account of the Kennedy brothers with Robert. Initially sidelined, even forgotten, because of his great age difference from his two

Psyche in Cross-Aspects: Thoughts on Synastry

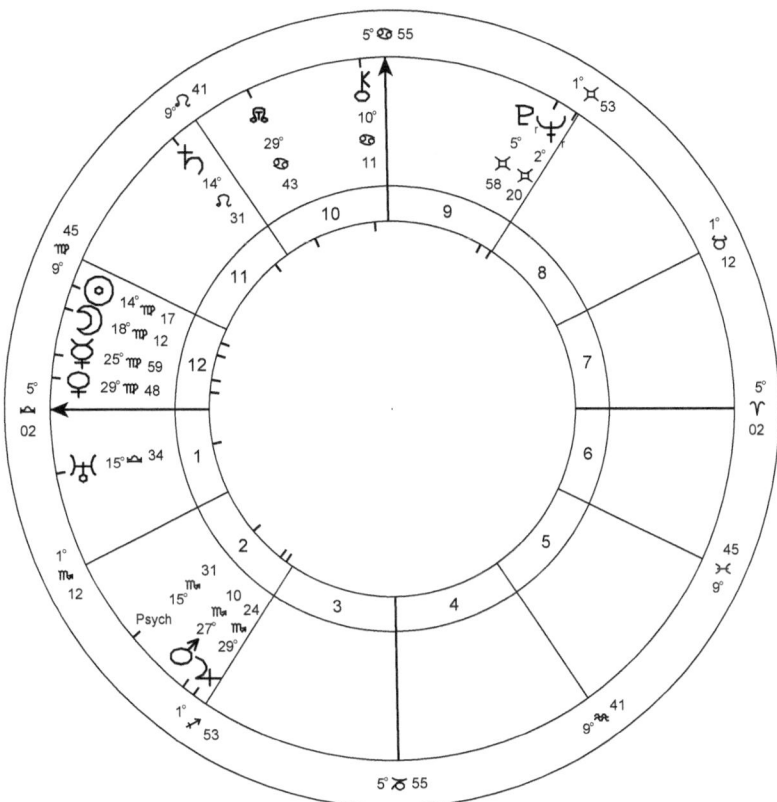

eldest siblings (he was ten years younger than Joe Jr.), he did everything he could to win his place in his father's plans, although he was more his mother's favourite because of his great sensitivity, linked to his stellium in Scorpio. It wasn't easy in a family of nine children, and Bobby had the impression of being completely invisible until Joe Jr's death, which made him number two in the order of succession. Thus, from the moment JFK declared his presidential ambitions, shortly after the death of his eldest brother, Robert became the man in the shadows, the Richelieu, the man who made himself indispensable but did not take credit. On their father's advice, JFK eventually appointed him Attorney General, a post in which Bobby led an open battle against the Mafia. As said earlier, after 22 November 1963 he still feared that he'd caused his brother's death by

174 In The Name of Love – The Asteroid Psyche

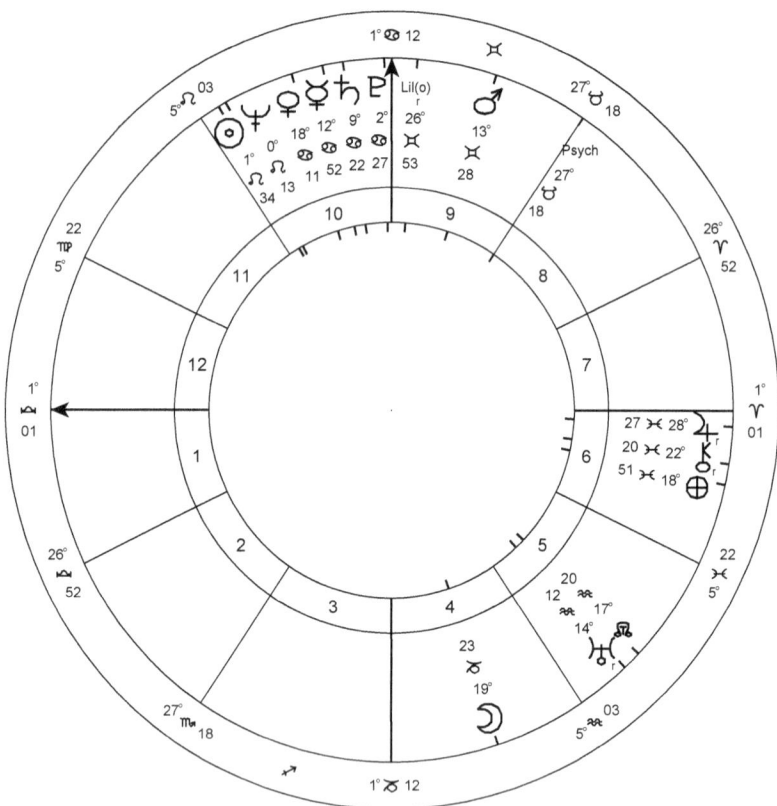

angering the wrong people. In the end, he too was sacrificed on the altar of the Kennedys' ambition, both out of a personal calling and to make up for his brother's death by continuing the fight that had probably cost him his life. The last son, Edward (Ted), could never really compete with his brothers, although he was also involved in politics. After Robert's assassination, he caused the death of a young woman in a car accident, from which his reputation never recovered. He was never a rival to his brothers because of the huge age difference between them.

In this masculine portrait of the Kennedy family, it's interesting to study the cross-aspects between the charts of the three brothers and of their father. From the outset, we can't help but notice the emphasis on the sign of Gemini and the cross-aspects involving Psyche. JFK's Sun and

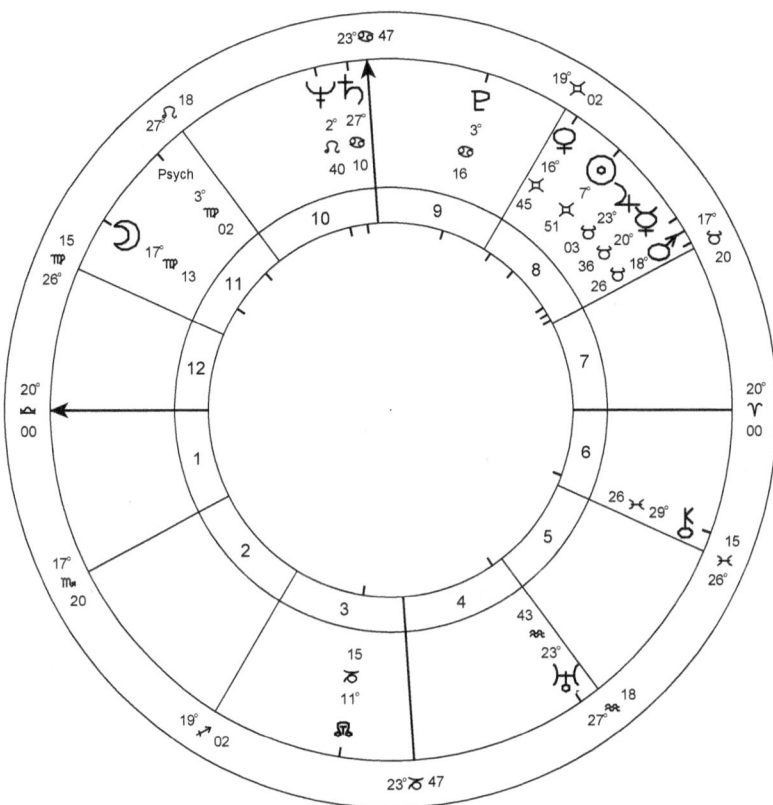

Venus are in Gemini, echoing his older brother's Mars in the same sign. For JFK, these planets are in the eighth house, and given the Mars symbolism, the theme of sibling rivalry is indeed a possibility suggested by this configuration. In his case, the eighth house was the theatre where this Gemini issue was played out: rivalry, jealousy, power struggles, domination – all against the background of a presumed paternal inheritance. Robert, for his part, had Psyche in Gemini, closely conjunct JFK's Sun and Joe Jr.'s Mars, which gives us a good idea of the role his two brothers and their aura played in Bobby's development. He was fascinated by JFK's Gemini intelligence and the physical and mental strength (Mars) of his Leo-born older brother, and his brothers were two Cupids activating his Psyche. Even after JFK's death, we can see that the phase of his life when he realised what he really wanted, which was to run for president, was at the moment of the quincunx of his progressed Sun to Psyche. He was still following the Sun of his brother, the president before him, as his inner guide, that of the beauty he'd once admired.

Looking at the chart of their father, Joe Sr, we see again what we saw with Queen Elizabeth II, who had cross-aspects between her Pluto and the Psyches of all her successors. Again, Joe Sr's Pluto, at 5°58 of Gemini, is conjunct the Psyches of Bobby and Joe Jr (the latter at the end of Taurus), and square those of JFK and Ted at the beginning of Virgo. We have seen that although this father genuinely loved his sons, their relationships were not without tension. The power symbolised by Pluto is the atmosphere in which his sons were brought up and, above all, in these families, self-knowledge comes from being clear about one's desire for power, one's propensity to endure it and its effects on the relationships forged in adulthood. Pluto, which also symbolises fate, suggests that for the Kennedy sons the quest for self is coloured by fatality, in other words by the familial transmission, by the relationship with their father. Self-knowledge (Psyche) and solar fulfilment must take account of the fact that, as with the heirs to the royal crown, they perceived and found fascinating the Plutonian beauty of their father.

As for the supportive but terribly oppressive role Joe Sr played in the development of his children, this is reflected by the square and the opposition between his Mars-Jupiter conjunction at the very end of Scorpio, and the Psyches of his two eldest children, JFK and Joe Jr. The same Mars-Jupiter conjunction also encircles Bobby's Sun, at 28° of Scorpio. Considering that this Mars-Jupiter conjunction is square Joe Sr.'s nodal axis, it's significant and helps us to understand the patriarch's boundless energy and optimism, as well as his quest for a dominant social position. As it's in aspect to the Psyches of the elders, his two heirs, it gives us an idea of how the boys must have felt in their relationship with this man inhabited by Mars and Jupiter who expected his sons to take up his torch. Their father was truly the Cupid who urged them to conquer the beauty of this Mars-Jupiter conjunction and try to make it their own, to be able to honour Venus and get a sense of worth.

Finally, Joe Jr's Psyche, at the end of Taurus, is conjunct JFK's Mercury-Mars conjunction. Although physically Joe always had the upper hand over the puny John, the latter was more brilliant, and Joe knew it. He'd confided to one of his sisters shortly before he died that he knew it would be John who would become president, because he was the most intelligent. This cross-aspect suggests that, in the eldest's self-development, it was his younger brother's intelligence and way of expressing himself that served as the spur that helped Joe Jr. try to appropriate his Psyche in Taurus.

Cross-aspects' pivotal role in unveiling Psyche's qualities

When our Psyche forms a close aspect to one of the planets in the chart of someone close to us, it's likely that this person embodies for us, in one way or another, a form of beauty we desire and triggers a need to unveil the qualities of our own Psyche. These qualities are always those of the sign of the asteroid in our birth chart, coloured by the planets to which she forms close aspects in our chart. The planet in play in the other person's chart shows how it can affect us: if our Psyche is conjunct their Jupiter, we may feel supported in revealing the qualities necessary to honour Venus and gain a sense of self-worth. If our Psyche is in aspect to their Saturn, these people may embody a tutor or demonstrate a righteousness or expertise that arouse our admiration and then our desire to unfold the same qualities in relationships. If these aspects are difficult, like squares, it seems that the person may not support our quest for the qualities symbolised by Psyche. They may not value themselves, or the relationship may be complicated, ambiguous, or supportive in some ways, but not in the way we need to do the work necessary to find our own beauty. Or we may feel the need to fight that person in order to conquer those qualities. And Cupid may seem to elude us.

The cross-aspects between two Psyches in synastry are also interesting: if the qualities we're meant to develop through our relationships are compatible with those of the other person (signs in trine or sextile, for example), our quests may echo each other. On the other hand, if the Psyches are square, for example, in Scorpio and Leo, while one seeks to find within oneself the beauty of the shadow and the understanding of what's going on behind the scenes, the other may need to come into the light and run the risk of self-expression. From then on there may be a fundamental incompatibility in the inner process of unveiling symbolised by Psyche, inner needs and desires may clash, and the relationship, though it may remain fruitful on many levels, may be frustrating (but potentially enlightening), from this point of view.

Conclusion

In the nineteenth century, just before the discovery of Psyche, the Romantic movement proposed a new vision of the union between a man and a woman, in which practical considerations and duty no longer took precedence. The ideal love has since become the love between two soulmates, living in total fulfilment through the fusion of bodies, hearts and souls. In many ways, this ideal continues to be conveyed in the twenty-first century, and there are many people who, without daring to admit it, are searching for such loving fulfilment.

Almost two thousand years ago, Apuleius had already tried to propose a new vision of love between a man and a woman, in a Roman Empire where, in the century before his birth, the Stoics had already tried to reconcile love and marriage. Plutarch, for his part, had extolled a marriage in which the spouses were virtuous, in the Platonic sense of the word, and respectful of each other. Plutarch, who died the same year Apuleius was born, valued marriage on all levels: emotional, moral and intellectual. Apuleius's vision came at a fertile time when other authors, such as Pliny the Younger, had already extolled the virtues of love and happiness in marriage. Although, as a disciple of Plato, his ultimate dream was that we could all achieve true happiness through love of the divine, Apuleius remained realistic and proposed to his fellow human beings a form of love that was certainly virtuous, but more easily attainable. However, he is very clear: this kind of love, the kind that brings us closer to the divine within us and at the same time allows us earthly happiness, *voluptas*, is only accessible after Venusian labours. By this he means work on ourselves, sometimes difficult and risky, aimed at expressing the Venusian function in a healthy way and enabling us to enter into a union in which we symbolically become immortal, for our Sun can find its place among the stars.

The development of psychoanalysis, which followed the discovery of Neptune (1846) and Psyche (1852), confirmed Apuleius's view: we're not naturally suited to happiness in marriage, and our choice of partner is not always genuine. The icy black waters of the third work and the kingdom of Proserpine in the fourth illustrate the links between the myth of Psyche and psychoanalytic theory. Wisdom, which enables us to make choices based on our values and to make our decisions according to what we have chosen, can also be seen as one of the goals of psychoanalytic work.

Any activation of the Psyche asteroid is therefore an opportune time to do or adjust whatever work is needed before a healthy relationship can be established, to examine what we need to change in ourselves before we ask anything of the other person. Of course, this work can also be done while we're already in a relationship, and it will then be conducive to a more or less significant change, depending on the nature and duration of the transit, in the way we relate to our partner and express our values within the couple.

Bibliography

Anselmini, Julie and Schopp, Claude, *Dumas amoureux* (Presses universitaires de Caen, 2020).

Apuleius, Lucius, *Apologia (The Defense of Apuleius)*, trans. by J. Arthur Hanson (Harvard University Press, 1962).

Apuleius, Lucius, *De Platone et eius dogmate* (Createspace Independent Publishing Platform, 2014).

Apuleius, Lucius, *The Golden Ass*, trans. E. J. Kenney (Penguin Classics, 1999).

Brandus, Paul, *Jackie, her Transformation from First Lady to Jackie O.* (Post Hill Press 2020).

Clayton, Tim and Craig, Philip, *Diana : Story of a Princess* (Simon & Schuster 2001).

De Beauvoir, Simone, *Diary of a Philosophy Student: Volume 3, 1926-30* (University of Illinois Press, 2024).

De Nerval, Gérard, *Aurélia, Sylvie, Les chimères* (Libertalia 2018).

De Stefano, Cristina, *The Child is The Teacher* (Other Press, 2022).

Dimbleby, Jonathan, *The Prince of Wales: A Biography* (Little, Brown, 1994).

Du Châtelet, Émilie, *La Correspondance d'Émilie Du Châtelet 1733-1740* (Centre international d'étude du XVIIIe siècle 2018).

Dulong, Claude, *Anne d'Autriche* (Hachette, 2000).

Farris, Scott. *Inga: Kennedy's Great Love, Hitler's Perfect Beauty, and J. Edgar Hoover's Prime Suspect* (Lyons Press 2016).

Ferenczi, Sándor. *Confusion of Tongues Between the Adults and the Child: The Language of Tenderness and of Passion*, trans. by Isabella S. K. Seiffert (Karnac Books, 1994).

Freud, Anna, *The Ego and the Mechanisms of Defence*, trans. by Cecil Baines (Hogarth Press, 1937).

Freud, Sigmund, *On Narcissism : An introduction, in The Standard Edition of the Complete Psychological Works of Sigmund Freud, Vol.14 (1914-1916)* (Hogarth Press 1957).

Geck, Martin, *Robert Schumann: The Life and Work of a Romantic Composer*, trans. Stewart Spencer (University of Chicago Press 2012).

Gidel, Henry, *Jackie Kennedy* (Flammarion, 2011).

Greene, Liz and Sasportas, Howard, *Dynamics of the Unconscious: Seminars in Psychology Astrology, Vol.2* (Red Wheel / Weiser, 1988).

Greene, Liz, *Relationships and How to Survive Them* (The Wessex Astrologer, 2023).

Gregor-Dellin, Martin, *Richard Wagner* (Fayard, 1981).

Haley, Alex, *The Autobiography of Malcolm X as told to Alex Haley* (Turtleback Books 1987).

Hardmann, John, *Marie-Antoinette : The Making of a French Queen* (Yale University Press, 2019).

Houssaye, Arsène, *Confessions d'un demi-siècle. 1830-1880, tome I* (Paris, E.Dentu, 1885; BnF collection ebooks, 2015).

Hugo, Victor, *Océan – Tas de pierres* (Albin Michel, 1942).

Lady Colin Campbell, *The Real Diana* (Arcadia Books, 2005).

Lever, Evelyne, *Marie-Antoinette, Correspondance, 1770-1793* (Tallandier 2006).

Montessori, Maria, *Maria Montessori Sails to America*, trans. and introduced by Carolina Montessori (Montessori-Pierson Publishing Company, 2013).

Nietzsche, Franziska, *Lettres de Franziska Nietzsche à Franz Overbeck, précédées des Billets de la folie de Friedrich Nietzsche,* trans.by Guillaume Ollendorff (Éditions Bouquins, 2023).

Nietzsche, Friedrich, *Ecce Homo: How One Becomes What One Is,* trans. by R. J. Hollingdale (Cambridge University Press, 1998).

Nietzsche, Friedrich, *Human, All Too Human,* trans. by R. J. Hollingdale (Cambridge University Press, 1986).

Nietzsche, Friedrich, *The Antichrist,* trans. by R. J. Hollingdale (Cambridge University Press, 1998).

Nietzsche, Friedrich, *The Case of Wagner,* trans. by R. J. Hollingdale (Cambridge University Press, 1998).

Nietzsche, Friedrich, *The Gay Science,* trans. by Walter Kaufmann (Cambridge University Press, 2001).

Nietzsche, Friedrich, *Untimely Meditations,* trans. by R. J. Hollingdale (Cambridge University Press, 1997).

Nietzsche, Friedrich, *Selected Letters of Friedrich Nietzsche*, ed. and trans. Christopher Middleton (University of Chicago Press, 1969).

Pinchot Michael, *Mary Mary and JFK* (Xlibris Corporation 2013).

Plato, *The Symposium* (Penguin Classics; Reissue edition 2003).

Preisendanz, Karl, *The Greek Magical Papyri in Translation Including the Demotic Spells (*PGM IV. 1716-1870. University of Chicago Press, 1986.).

Proust, Marcel, *Contre Sainte-Beuve* (Gallimard, coll. Bibliothèque de la Pléiade, 1971).

Proust, Marcel, *Correspondance de Marcel Proust, tome V* (Plon. 1979, p.345).

Proust, Marcel, *In Search of Lost Time* (Everyman, 2001).

Proust, Marcel, *lettre à Ladilslas Landowski, Correspondance de Marcel Proust, tome VI* (Plon. 1979, p.110).

Proust, Marcel, *Time Regained. In Search of Lost Time Vol. VI* (Modern Library 2003).

Rudhyar, Dane, *An Astrological Study of Psychological Complexes* (Shambhala 1976).

Rudhyar, Dane, *New Mansions for New Men* (Borodino Books 2017).

Sarmant, Thierry, *Homme et roi* (Tallandier 2014).

Sasportas, Howard, *Direction and Destiny in the Birth Chart* (The Wessex Astrologer, 2023).

Schumann, Clara and Robert, *The Diary of Robert and Clara Schumann* (Koehler und Amelang, 1934).

Snégaroff, Thomas, *Kennedy: Une vie en clair-obscur* (Paris: Armand Colin, 2013).

Sylla, Fodé and Sbigniew Kowalevski, *Qui a peur de Malcolm X ?* (Éditions Ramsay, 1993).

Thatcher, Margaret, *The Path to Power* (HarperCollins 1995).

The Beatles, *The Beatles Anthology* (Chronicle Books, 2000).

Thomas, Evan, *Robert Kennedy: his life* (Simon & Schuster 2002).

Voltaire, *"Mémoires pour servir à la vie de Monsieur de Voltaire" in Œuvres complètes de Voltaire*, ed. Beuchot, Vol. I (Garnier Frères, 1883, p.7).

Von Franz, Marie-Louise, *The Golden Ass of Apuleius: The Liberation of the Feminine in Man* (C. G. Jung Foundation Books Series, 2001).

Wagner, Cosima, *Cosima Wagner's Diaries, Vol. 2: 1878-1883* (A Helen and Kurt Wolff Book/Harcourt Brace Jovanovich, 1978).

Wenner. Jann S., *Lennon remembers: The Full Rolling Stone Interviews from 1970* (New York: Verso, 2000).

Whiteside, Derek T., *The Preliminary Manuscript for Isaac Newton's 1687 Principia, 1684-1685* (Cambridge University Press, 1989).

Zweig, Stefan, *Marie Antoinette: The Portrait of an Average Woman*, trans. from German by Eden et Cedar Paul (Viking Press, 1933).

About the Author

Anne-Marie Chabellard holds a PhD in biological sciences and has always nurtured a keen interest in research and experimentation. She also earned a degree in psychology and went on to pursue a career in teaching. At the same time, she has been studying astrology for over twenty years, beginning with Jungian psychological astrology before expanding her studies to other astrological traditions, including classical ones. More recently, she has developed a particular passion for asteroids, which she has been researching for several years with a focus on validating her insights through experience. She lives and consults in Paris, France.

www.ingramcontent.com/pod-product-compliance
Lightning Source LLC
Chambersburg PA
CBHW062046220426

43662CB00010B/1672